CONFIDENCE AT WORK

Overcome Insecurity and Succeed at the Workplace

I0465506

Confidence at work - Overcoming Insecurity and Succeed at the Workplace

Published by Angel Marqués Sánchez
ISBN: 9798300624736

Hello! I would greatly appreciate it if you could share your opinion by leaving a review on Amazon. Reviews not only help other readers discover the book, but they're also essential for supporting future projects.

If you have a few minutes, please visit the review page by scanning the QR code below.

When Priya stepped into the boardroom for her first presentation as a newly promoted manager, the hum of side conversations and the shuffle of papers were nearly deafening. She clutched her notes tightly, her knuckles whitening against the polished pages she had rehearsed a dozen times the night before. Her outfit was impeccable, her slides flawless, and her data meticulously triple-checked. Still, an unshakable voice in her head whispered doubts: *What if they think I'm not ready for this role? What if I stumble on a question?*

The meeting began, and Priya's turn to speak arrived all too quickly. Her heart raced as she introduced her project updates, her voice steady but her tone reserved. As she advanced through her slides, she noticed subtle signs—a colleague's raised eyebrow, a glance exchanged between senior team members. To her, these gestures weren't neutral; they were judgments, confirmations of the inadequacy she already feared. Though the room offered no direct criticism, Priya's words grew quieter, her pace quicker, her confidence dwindling with every passing minute.

After she finished, the silence in the room felt heavier than applause. The team leader nodded curtly and moved on to the next agenda item without much comment. A flush of relief mixed with disappointment swept over Priya as she sank back into her chair. She had survived the presentation, but something felt missing. She replayed the meeting in her mind, focusing on every potential flaw: the part where she stumbled over a statistic, the lack of energy in her delivery. She wondered if she should have spent even more time preparing or if she was truly unqualified for this new position.

Later that afternoon, her manager approached her in the hallway. "You covered the basics, but next time, don't hold back. I know you have great insights, but you need to show them," he said with a smile that was meant to reassure. For Priya, though, the comment hit like a spotlight on her insecurity. She realized she hadn't just held back ideas—she'd held back herself. The opportunity to demonstrate her leadership, to own her expertise, had been right in front of her, and she had let it slip by, trapped in the confines of her own doubt.

This was far from the last time Priya faced such moments, but it was a turning point. It forced her to confront a truth she hadn't fully admitted to herself: her insecurity wasn't protecting her from failure—it was silently sabotaging her success.

Define insecurity in the workplace

Insecurity in the workplace often operates in the shadows, subtly influencing decisions, shaping behaviors, and creating barriers that many professionals may not even realize exist. It manifests in quiet moments—the hesitation to speak up during a meeting, the urge to triple-check an email before sending it, or the nagging feeling of inadequacy despite a proven track record of success. While it might seem like a personal struggle, it's a nearly universal experience, cutting across industries, career stages, and hierarchies.

Fundamentally, workplace insecurity stems from the fear of not meeting expectations—whether imposed by others or self-imposed. This fear can loom large in a world where performance is constantly measured, achievements are publicly displayed, and comparisons are unavoidable. In today's fast-paced and competitive work environments, even high achievers can fall prey to doubts about their competence, worthiness, or ability to keep up.

Despite its prevalence, self-doubt often remains unspoken, camouflaged by outward displays of confidence or masked by overwork. It doesn't announce itself loudly but whispers persistently, shaping how people perceive their capabilities and limiting their willingness to take risks or embrace opportunities. Left unchecked, these feelings can become a silent saboteur, holding individuals back from realizing their potential and cultivating fulfilling professional lives.

By understanding the roots and manifestations of this doubt, professionals can begin to break free from its grip. This section sets the stage for identifying how such feelings affect not only individual career trajectories but also the broader dynamics of teams and organizations. Recognizing this issue as both personal and systemic is the first step toward reclaiming control and building resilience in the workplace.

Workplace self-doubt is the persistent feeling of inadequacy in one's professional abilities, role, or worth. It stems from the fear of failure, rejection, or criticism in a setting where performance and results are constantly evaluated. This feeling can manifest as an internalized belief that one is not "good enough" or fears being exposed as unqualified, even when evidence suggests otherwise.

At its core, workplace self-doubt is deeply tied to the psychological mechanisms of self-perception and external validation. It often originates from feelings of inadequacy, shaped by past experiences, societal expectations, or a lack of confidence in one's skills. For example, an employee may hesitate to volunteer for a leadership role, not because they lack the capability, but because they fear scrutiny or failure. This fear can create a cycle of underperformance, reinforcing feelings of inadequacy and perpetuating the doubt.

However, insecurity is not always self-generated. The workplace environment itself can amplify these feelings. Competitive cultures, unclear expectations, or inconsistent feedback can leave individuals questioning their value and contributions. Implicit biases and microaggressions, particularly in diverse workplaces, can exacerbate feelings of inadequacy, making individuals from marginalized groups feel unwelcome or underqualified.

Workplace self-doubt isn't simply a personal flaw; it's a complex interplay of internal fears and external pressures. Understanding its nuanced definition helps to highlight that these feelings are not rare or isolated. Instead, they are part of a broader challenge that, when addressed, can unlock personal growth and professional fulfillment. This definition sets the foundation for exploring how these feelings manifest and the tools needed to confront them.

MANIFESTATIONS IN PROFESSIONAL LIFE

Workplace insecurity reveals itself in diverse ways, often blending seamlessly into daily professional behaviors, making it challenging to recognize. It can range from subtle hesitations to more overt patterns that influence career progression and workplace relationships. These manifestations often stem from the underlying fear of judgment, failure, or inadequacy, shaping how individuals approach challenges and interact with their environment.

One of the most common manifestations is perfectionism—an unrelenting desire to meet impossibly high standards as a way to compensate for perceived shortcomings. Employees might overwork themselves, spending hours refining reports or rechecking emails, driven by the fear of criticism. While this can initially appear as diligence, it often leads to burnout, reduced productivity, and dissatisfaction when the effort goes unnoticed. Insecure professionals may avoid situations that put their abilities in the spotlight. This can include declining leadership opportunities, avoiding challenging projects, or hesitating to voice opinions in meetings. By playing it safe, they limit their exposure to failure but also miss out on growth opportunities, which reinforces the insecurity.

Some individuals rely heavily on external validation to counter their feelings of inadequacy. They may seek constant feedback, approval, or reassurance from colleagues and supervisors. While this can momentarily boost confidence, it creates a dependency on others' opinions rather than fostering self-assurance, leaving individuals vulnerable to criticism or perceived neglect.

Comparing oneself to others is another hallmark of workplace insecurity. Social media platforms like LinkedIn exacerbate this, presenting curated success stories that can make individuals feel inadequate. Comparing achievements, roles, or even work styles to peers often leads to feelings of inferiority, despite personal successes.

Insecure employees often struggle with receiving feedback, viewing it as confirmation of their inadequacies rather than an opportunity for growth. Similarly, they may avoid addressing conflicts or difficult conversations out of fear that they will be judged or disliked. This can erode professional relationships and hinder team dynamics.

These manifestations are not isolated incidents but often interwoven into broader workplace patterns, impacting performance, satisfaction, and career progression. By identifying these behaviors, individuals can take the first step toward addressing and overcoming insecurity, enabling them to engage more authentically and confidently in their professional lives.

WORKPLACE DYNAMICS AND CULTURAL INFLUENCE

Workplace insecurity is not solely an individual challenge—it is shaped and amplified by the dynamics and culture of the professional environment. A company's norms, values, and interactions can either help alleviate feelings of inadequacy or deepen them, depending on how they address—or fail to address—key factors such as inclusivity, feedback systems, and organizational pressures.

In workplaces where competition is prioritized over collaboration, these feelings can thrive. Employees may feel the need to constantly prove their worth to outperform peers, leading to heightened anxiety and a fear of failure. Such environments foster a "survival of the fittest" mentality, where perceived weaknesses are magnified, and support systems are limited. The pressure to achieve can transform these feelings into a persistent undercurrent, discouraging risk-taking and innovation.

A lack of clarity in roles, expectations, or performance criteria is another significant driver of insecurity. When employees are uncertain about what success looks like or how their work is evaluated, they may question their contributions and worth. Ambiguity in feedback—such as vague or inconsistent appraisals—can exacerbate this, leaving individuals feeling unmoored and undervalued.

For employees from marginalized backgrounds, insecurity is often compounded by biases and systemic inequities embedded in workplace cultures. Microaggressions, whether intentional or unintentional, signal exclusion and perpetuate doubts about belonging. Implicit biases in hiring, promotions, or project assignments can leave individuals feeling overlooked, reinforcing feelings of inadequacy and alienation. Leaders play a pivotal role in shaping workplace dynamics. Authoritarian or overly critical leadership can instill fear of failure, discouraging open communication and experimentation. Conversely, empathetic and inclusive leaders can foster a culture where employees feel supported and secure in expressing themselves. The tone set by leadership trickles down, influencing how insecurity is addressed—or ignored—across the organization.

In an increasingly connected world, workplace culture extends beyond the physical office. Platforms like LinkedIn often showcase idealized professional achievements, creating unrealistic benchmarks and fueling insecurity among employees who feel they fall short. This "highlight reel" culture can skew perceptions of success and amplify feelings of inadequacy, particularly in industries where personal branding is emphasized.

Workplace dynamics and cultural influences are not just backdrops to insecurity—they actively shape how it emerges and evolves. Addressing these factors requires intentional efforts to build environments that prioritize transparency, inclusivity, and psychological safety. By understanding how external forces contribute to insecurity, organizations can create cultures that empower employees to thrive.

BROADER IMPACTS ON THE INDIVIDUAL

The ripple effects of workplace self-doubt extend far beyond professional performance, influencing the emotional, psychological, and even physical well-being of individuals. These impacts often intertwine, creating a feedback loop that reinforces these feelings and their consequences, both inside and outside the workplace.

Workplace insecurity often manifests as chronic uncertainty, driving a constant fear of judgment or failure. This persistent state of anxiety can lead to emotional exhaustion, where the individual feels overwhelmed and unable to cope with daily challenges. Over time, these emotions can erode self-esteem, leaving individuals questioning their value not only at work but in other areas of life.

Insecurity in the workplace often spills into professional and personal relationships. Colleagues may perceive insecure behaviors—such as over-apologizing, reluctance to contribute, or defensiveness—as signs of distrust or lack of confidence. This can strain team dynamics, leading to miscommunication or a sense of isolation. Outside of work, the emotional strain caused by workplace insecurity can result in withdrawal from friends and family, further deepening the sense of alienation.

Professionally, the broader impacts of uncertainty are most visible in stagnation. Fear of failure or rejection can deter individuals from pursuing promotions, negotiating salaries, or taking on leadership roles. This hesitancy to advocate for oneself can result in missed opportunities, reinforcing the cycle of self-doubt and limiting professional development.

The stress associated with workplace uncertainty can take a significant toll on physical health. Prolonged stress can contribute to sleep disturbances, headaches, and other psychosomatic symptoms. In severe cases, it may even lead to chronic conditions such as hypertension or weakened immunity. Mentally, individuals may experience burnout or depression, particularly when this inner turmoil is paired with high job demands and low perceived support.

When this pervasive unease dominates one's professional life, it often overshadows the sense of purpose and satisfaction derived from meaningful work. Tasks that once felt engaging or rewarding may become sources of stress, diminishing overall job satisfaction. Over time, this diminished fulfillment can lead to a loss of motivation, disengagement, or even a complete career shift.

These broader impacts underscore the urgency of addressing workplace insecurity at its root. By recognizing how deeply it affects individuals on multiple levels, professionals and organizations can work together to create strategies that prioritize well-being and resilience, ensuring that these feelings do not define one's professional identity or potential.

THE HIDDEN EROSION OF IDENTITY AND AMBITION

Workplace insecurity often works insidiously, gradually eroding an individual's sense of identity and personal ambition. This phenomenon is subtle but profound, as it undermines the confidence needed to navigate not just professional challenges but life itself. When insecurity becomes a dominant lens through which individuals view their abilities, they may start to internalize their perceived shortcomings as immutable aspects of who they are.

This erosion of identity can manifest as a reluctance to dream big or take risks. Ambitions that once felt achievable might shrink under the weight of self-doubt, replaced by an emphasis on mere survival or the avoidance of failure. This shift not only narrows career possibilities but also diminishes the personal satisfaction derived from striving toward meaningful goals.

In many cases, the internal narrative shaped by workplace insecurity becomes self-reinforcing. Negative self-perceptions feed a fear of judgment or rejection, leading individuals to shy away from opportunities that could challenge these beliefs. Over time, this cycle of avoidance and diminished self-worth can strip away the sense of agency that is vital for personal and professional growth.

The long-term impact of this erosion goes beyond the workplace, affecting how individuals see themselves in broader contexts—whether as partners, parents, or members of their communities. The loss of confidence and ambition does not remain confined to office walls; it influences the choices individuals make and the risks they are willing to take in every facet of life. Addressing workplace insecurity, therefore, is not just about professional success but also about preserving the integrity of one's identity and the courage to pursue a fulfilling future.

Highlight its hidden impact on career growth, job satisfaction, and professional relationships

The whispers of insecurity often go unheard, hidden beneath layers of polished professionalism and daily routine. Yet, it lingers, shaping decisions and altering perceptions in ways many fail to notice until it has already left its mark. The workplace, a realm often idealized as a space for growth and collaboration, becomes a stage where insecurity crafts quiet barriers to success. Its impacts are subtle, rarely announced with bold declarations, but rather woven into the smallest hesitations, the softest doubts. Before one knows it, it has set a ceiling on what seems achievable.

Consider a moment when a promising idea was left unsaid in a meeting, not because it lacked merit but because fear whispered that it might not be good enough. Or recall a time when an opportunity was passed over, not for lack of desire but for a gnawing worry about inadequacy. These moments accumulate, shaping careers not by external failures but by the internal battles we fight and, too often, lose. Insecurity, though rarely discussed, becomes the invisible thread linking stalled promotions, unmet goals, and a gnawing sense of discontent.

What makes this feeling so insidious is its ability to operate in the background, subtly dictating choices and influencing relationships. Unlike overt challenges, it rarely announces itself, making it easy to dismiss or ignore. Many professionals rationalize its presence, attributing their decisions to external circumstances or timing. In reality, insecurity wields a subtle power, influencing how individuals see themselves and how they believe others see them. Left unchecked, it creates a feedback loop where small doubts grow into significant barriers.

By framing self-questioning as a hidden antagonist, this book aims to uncover its nuanced effects on professional life. Its goal is not to place blame but to shine a light on the ways such doubts infiltrate career growth, job satisfaction, and relationships, often without our conscious awareness. This journey is not just about identifying the problem but also about reclaiming control, empowering individuals to face these concerns head-on and break the cycle. Recognizing the hidden influence of these underlying fears is the first step toward achieving a fulfilling and impactful professional life.

CAREER GROWTH: THE INVISIBLE CEILING

In the labyrinth of professional advancement, insecurity often acts as an unseen architect, designing barriers that limit potential. It doesn't announce itself with bold declarations; rather, it whispers doubts into moments of decision-making. Promotions are missed not because the qualifications are lacking but because insecurity plants the idea that one isn't ready or worthy. Opportunities for leadership are declined as fear of failure overshadows the possibility of success. Over time, these seemingly small hesitations build an invisible ceiling that defines how high one believes they can climb.

This ceiling is rarely challenged directly, as internalized fears shape the narrative individuals tell themselves about their capabilities.. When a colleague is promoted, the insecure professional may not see it as a reflection of different circumstances or opportunities but as evidence of their own inadequacy. This internalized comparison becomes a constant source of self-doubt, diminishing the ability to advocate for oneself. The individual becomes their harshest critic, scrutinizing every performance and interpreting constructive feedback as confirmation of their perceived shortcomings.

Organizations inadvertently reinforce this ceiling by rewarding confidence as much as competence. Those who project assurance are often entrusted with opportunities and roles they may not yet fully master, while those hesitant to assert themselves are overlooked. This creates a self-perpetuating cycle, where reluctance to engage is mistaken for a lack of ambition or capability. In environments that value boldness, this hesitation can become a subtle yet significant disadvantage.

The cost of this invisible ceiling extends beyond individual limitations, affecting the entire organization. Missed opportunities for innovation, untapped talent, and unvoiced ideas represent growth potential left on the table. Breaking this cycle requires a deeper understanding of how these limiting behaviors manifest and finding ways to actively counteract them. By recognizing the role of these unspoken barriers, individuals and organizations can work together to dismantle this ceiling and cultivate a culture of opportunity and advancement.

JOB SATISFACTION: THE SILENT EROSION

Insecurity in the workplace has a way of quietly chipping away at job satisfaction, often without individuals realizing the full extent of its influence. It manifests as a persistent undercurrent, distorting perceptions and undermining a sense of accomplishment. Tasks that should bring pride are overshadowed by nagging doubts, and milestones feel hollow because insecurity whispers that success was luck, not skill. Over time, this inner dialogue erodes the joy and fulfillment that work can bring, leaving individuals disconnected from their achievements.

The nature of insecurity makes it particularly insidious in how it reshapes one's relationship with work. When plagued by self-questioning, even constructive feedback can feel like criticism, and neutral interactions are often interpreted through a lens of judgment.

This creates a heightened sensitivity to perceived slights, fostering a defensive or withdrawn demeanor. What might have been an engaging and collaborative environment begins to feel fraught with tension, not because of external hostility but because of the internal battles being waged.

This erosion doesn't just affect day-to-day satisfaction; it also influences how individuals view their roles within an organization. Insecurity often leads to a disproportionate focus on weaknesses, overshadowing strengths and contributions. When employees believe they are falling short, they may disengage from their work, avoiding challenges or opportunities for fear of failure. This disengagement creates a feedback loop, where lack of enthusiasm reinforces the belief that they are unfit for their role, further diminishing satisfaction and motivation.

Left unchecked, the erosion of job satisfaction caused by insecurity can have broader consequences. It contributes to burnout, lowers productivity, and increases turnover rates, both for the individual and the organization. Yet this decline is not inevitable. By recognizing insecurity's subtle role in undermining satisfaction, individuals can learn to challenge these narratives and reconnect with the aspects of their work that once brought purpose and joy. Job satisfaction, like confidence, can be rebuilt—but it requires an honest appraisal of the factors that quietly wear it away.

PROFESSIONAL RELATIONSHIPS: FRAGILE CONNECTIONS

Insecurity subtly infiltrates professional relationships, undermining trust, collaboration, and the ability to connect authentically with colleagues. It often introduces an unspoken barrier between individuals, fostering doubt about one's place in a team or how others perceive them. This sense of fragility creates a defensive posture, where interactions are carefully curated to minimize vulnerability, and genuine connections are sacrificed for the sake of self-preservation. Over time, these fragile connections can weaken the social fabric essential for workplace success.

One way insecurity manifests in relationships is through overcompensation or withdrawal. Some individuals, feeling the need to prove their worth, may dominate conversations, overpromise on deliverables, or attempt to micromanage tasks. While these behaviors stem from a desire to demonstrate value, they can come across as controlling or dismissive, alienating colleagues. On the other hand, insecurity may lead to avoidance—hesitating to speak up in meetings, share ideas, or take ownership of projects. Both responses hinder collaboration, as they either stifle input or overshadow the contributions of others.

The impact of insecurity extends beyond direct interactions to how individuals interpret others' actions. A neutral comment or constructive criticism can feel like a personal attack, fostering resentment or mistrust. Over time, these misinterpretations create a narrative that others are adversaries rather than allies. This misaligned perception erodes the mutual respect and openness needed for strong professional relationships, leaving individuals feeling isolated even in team-oriented environments.

Fragile connections also influence how support networks function in the workplace. Individuals who struggle with self-doubt may hesitate to seek help or mentorship, fearing it will expose their perceived inadequacies. This reluctance to reach out can result in missed opportunities for growth and insight. Moreover, colleagues may misinterpret this hesitancy as aloofness or disinterest, further widening the relational divide. Yet, professional relationships thrive on vulnerability, shared goals, and mutual encouragement—all of which are undermined when uncertainty dominates the dynamic.

Restoring strength to these connections requires a concerted effort to confront the role of self-questioning in shaping interactions. By fostering self-awareness and challenging internalized fears, individuals can engage with colleagues more authentically, cultivating relationships rooted in trust and collaboration. These efforts not only enhance individual confidence but also fortify the collective potential of the workplace.

THE INTERCONNECTED IMPACT: A VICIOUS CYCLE

Insecurity in the workplace does not operate in isolation; its effects are deeply intertwined, creating a self-perpetuating cycle that reinforces its grip. Career growth, job satisfaction, and professional relationships are not separate domains but interconnected facets of professional life, each influencing the others in profound ways. When insecurity takes root in one area, its ripples often extend to the rest, making it a pervasive force that feeds on itself.

For instance, insecurity might first manifest as hesitancy to pursue a promotion, driven by fears of inadequacy. This reluctance hampers career growth, leading to missed opportunities that further validate feelings of stagnation or incompetence. The absence of progress then impacts job satisfaction, as individuals begin to feel trapped in roles that no longer inspire or challenge them. The growing sense of dissatisfaction spills over into relationships, where interactions with colleagues become strained, either through withdrawal or overcompensating to mask perceived shortcomings. Each of these dynamics reinforces the others, creating a feedback loop that deepens insecurity.

This interconnected nature makes these challenges particularly difficult to address. A setback in one area—such as negative feedback during a performance review—can trigger a ripple effect. Confidence in professional abilities may falter, leading individuals to avoid new challenges, which, in turn, limits career advancement. Simultaneously, strained relationships can reduce access to the social support needed to rebuild assurance. The result is a cycle where hesitation and self-restriction become both the cause and consequence of professional struggles, reinforcing the barriers to growth and making it harder to break free.

The vicious cycle is not only damaging on an individual level but also creates broader organizational challenges. Teams affected by insecurity-driven dynamics often struggle with reduced collaboration, diminished innovation, and increased turnover. Insecure employees may hesitate to share bold ideas or challenge flawed decisions, fearing judgment or failure. This reluctance stifles creativity and limits the team's ability to adapt and excel. Over time, the collective impact of individual insecurities can erode the culture of an organization, making it less resilient and less cohesive.

Breaking this cycle requires recognizing its interconnected nature and addressing self-doubt holistically. Focusing on one area in isolation—whether it's career growth, job satisfaction, or relationships—may offer temporary relief but won't dismantle the broader system reinforcing the underlying fears. True progress lies in confronting self-doubt from multiple perspectives, empowering individuals to rebuild confidence while fostering an environment that supports growth, fulfillment, and connection. Only then can the cycle be reversed, transforming uncertainty from a limiting force into an opportunity for profound personal and professional development.

A CALL TO AWARENESS AND ACTION

Awareness is the first step in confronting the pervasive influence of workplace uncertainty. Too often, these feelings are dismissed as personal weaknesses or inevitable aspects of professional life, yet their impact extends far beyond the individual, subtly shaping the dynamics of teams, organizations, and even industries. Recognizing this uncertainty as a significant barrier to growth and satisfaction is not merely about self-help; it is about cultivating healthier workplaces that empower individuals and unlock collective potential.

This form of uncertainty thrives in silence. Left unaddressed, it perpetuates cycles of hesitation, missed opportunities, and strained relationships. Breaking this silence requires creating spaces where conversations about these challenges can occur without fear of judgment or dismissal.

For individuals, this means reflecting on personal triggers and patterns, understanding how they influence decisions and behaviors. For organizations, it demands a culture shift—acknowledging that insecurity is not a personal failing but a shared challenge shaped by structural, cultural, and interpersonal factors.

Action begins with intentional steps to dismantle the stigma surrounding self-doubt. Leaders and managers hold a critical role in fostering environments where vulnerability is seen as a strength rather than a liability. By modeling transparency—such as sharing their own experiences of overcoming uncertainty—they normalize these feelings and encourage others to seek support. Organizations must also invest in tools and training to help employees identify and address these feelings, such as mentorship programs, workshops on self-advocacy, and resources for mental well-being.

For individuals, the journey from hesitation to empowerment is deeply personal but not solitary. Seeking feedback, cultivating resilience, and building networks of trust are pivotal steps in reclaiming confidence. Equally important is reframing failure and rejection as inevitable aspects of growth rather than as definitive judgments of worth. Each step taken to confront limiting beliefs not only strengthens the individual but contributes to a broader cultural shift, where confidence is nurtured collectively and success is no longer constrained by silent fears.

This book is both a guide and a call to action. It invites readers to confront the hidden forces shaping their careers, to challenge the beliefs that hold them back, and to embrace a future defined by growth, fulfillment, and connection. Insecurity may be a silent career killer, but awareness and action can transform it into a catalyst for profound personal and professional change. The time to act is now, not just for ourselves but for the healthier, more dynamic workplaces we aspire to create.

Unlocking Potential for Lasting Success

Insecurity in the workplace is often shrouded in silence, a quiet undercurrent that many feel but few openly discuss. For most professionals, the experience of lack of confidence can emerge in countless ways: a hesitation before speaking in a meeting, the sinking feeling of not measuring up to peers, or the lingering question of whether one truly deserves a role or promotion. These feelings, far from being isolated to a select few, are deeply embedded in the human experience of striving within competitive, hierarchical environments. What makes insecurity particularly challenging is its ability to disguise itself, often hiding behind behaviors like overworking, perfectionism, or the relentless pursuit of external validation. By not addressing its presence, individuals inadvertently allow it to seep into their actions, decisions, and relationships.

Recognizing the universality of insecurity is a critical first step in disarming its hold. It is a shared experience, not a personal failing, and its roots are as varied as the people who encounter it. Some may trace these feelings to childhood environments where praise was scarce, while others may find them amplified by societal expectations or workplace cultures that prioritize results over individual well-being. Regardless of their origin, these challenges are often exacerbated by external pressures—the unrelenting demand to succeed, to innovate, and to constantly prove one's worth. These pressures are especially potent in today's fast-paced, hyper-visible professional landscape, where achievements are often broadcasted and compared across platforms like LinkedIn.

Importantly, acknowledging the challenge of these feelings does not mean resigning oneself to their effects. Instead, it is about reframing the narrative—seeing these emotions not as an indictment of one's worth but as a natural reaction to environments that test the boundaries of comfort and capability. Just as muscles grow stronger when exposed to resistance, so too can individuals grow when they confront and work through these challenges. By shining a light on the prevalence of these emotions, it becomes easier to detach them from the shame or stigma they often carry.

This acknowledgment also paves the way for empathy—not just toward oneself but also toward others. Recognizing that insecurity is universal fosters a sense of solidarity, breaking the illusion that everyone else has it all figured out. In a culture that often rewards confidence, even when it's performative, it's vital to remember that vulnerability is a shared human trait. Understanding this can help readers feel less alone in their struggles and more equipped to take the first steps toward addressing them. Through this lens, insecurity becomes less of a personal weakness and more of a shared challenge, one that can be tackled with honesty, courage, and the right tools.

DEFINING EMPOWERMENT AND ITS ROLE IN SUCCESS

Empowerment is often invoked as a motivational ideal, a rallying cry to take control of one's life and career. Yet, its true meaning extends far beyond a feel-good concept. Essentially, empowerment is the process of gaining confidence, authority, and control over one's decisions and actions. It involves the recognition of one's abilities, the willingness to take risks, and the capacity to navigate obstacles with resilience. In the context of the workplace, empowerment is both a mindset and a skill set—a combination of self-belief and the practical tools necessary to overcome insecurity and achieve success.

Insecurity thrives on self-doubt, convincing individuals that their worth hinges on external validation or avoiding failure. Empowerment challenges this narrative, reframing success as an active pursuit rooted in self-awareness and agency. It shifts the focus from what others think to what one is capable of achieving, fostering a sense of ownership over one's career trajectory. Empowered individuals recognize their inherent value and understand that setbacks are part of the journey, not an indictment of their worth.

The role of empowerment in addressing these challenges is transformative. It builds confidence, creating a foundation that enables individuals to take calculated risks and embrace opportunities. This transformation is gradual; it requires intentional effort to identify and unlearn limiting beliefs that restrict growth. Empowerment promotes introspection, guiding individuals to confront internal narratives that hinder progress. By doing so, it paves the way for a more fulfilling professional life, where confidence becomes the driving force, unlocking potential and inspiring action.

Moreover, empowerment is not merely a personal victory—it is a dynamic force that shapes workplace environments and relationships. Empowered individuals contribute more effectively to their teams, advocate for themselves and others, and model the kind of self-assurance that inspires colleagues. In this sense, empowerment becomes contagious; when individuals learn to claim their power, they create ripple effects that uplift those around them. This collective empowerment fosters a culture of collaboration and mutual support, replacing the fear-driven dynamics of insecurity with an atmosphere of trust and shared growth.

To achieve success, empowerment must be recognized not as an abstract goal but as a daily practice. It requires consistent effort to cultivate self-belief, align actions with values, and push through the discomfort that comes with growth. While insecurity feeds on hesitation and inaction, empowerment thrives on movement—on the courage to take the next step, no matter how small. Through this lens, success is not a distant destination but a series of empowered choices that accumulate over time, building a career grounded in confidence, resilience, and purpose.

THE TRANSFORMATIONAL JOURNEY

The path from insecurity to empowerment is rarely linear, often marked by setbacks, hesitation, and moments of vulnerability. Yet, it is precisely these challenges that define the transformational journey. Recognizing uncertainty or hesitation as a temporary state rather than a defining trait is the first step in initiating this shift. It requires understanding that growth is a process, one that involves unlearning limiting beliefs and adopting empowering perspectives. Transformation begins when individuals stop viewing these challenges as weaknesses and start seeing them as opportunities to cultivate strength and resilience.

Every transformational journey involves a pivotal moment—a realization or event that compels change. This might be a missed opportunity that sparks reflection, feedback from a trusted mentor, or the growing dissatisfaction with staying in one's comfort zone. These moments serve as catalysts, forcing individuals to confront the gap between where they are and where they aspire to be. Acknowledging this gap is not an admission of failure but an act of courage, a declaration that change is not only necessary but possible.

The journey toward empowerment often involves adopting new habits and mindsets that challenge the status quo. For instance, it might mean replacing negative self-talk with affirmations rooted in reality, focusing on achievements rather than perceived shortcomings. It could involve taking deliberate steps to build confidence, such as setting small, attainable goals that foster a sense of accomplishment. Over time, these practices accumulate, reshaping not only how individuals see themselves but also how they interact with the world around them. The process is transformative because it is deeply personal, requiring individuals to redefine their relationship with fear, failure, and self-worth.

A key aspect of this transformation is the ability to navigate discomfort. Insecurity thrives in safe, familiar spaces, discouraging risks and perpetuating self-doubt. Empowerment, on the other hand, demands stepping into the unknown, where growth occurs. This might mean advocating for oneself in a meeting, pursuing a promotion, or venturing into a new industry. Each act of courage, no matter how small, reinforces the belief that one is capable of more than insecurity allows them to imagine. The journey is less about erasing fear and more about learning to move forward despite it.

The transformational journey is not just about personal growth; it's about creating a life and career aligned with one's values and aspirations.

Empowerment transforms doubt into a stepping stone rather than an obstacle, enabling individuals to approach their goals with clarity and determination. The journey is ongoing, a continuous cycle of reflection, action, and adaptation. Yet, every step forward is a testament to the individual's capacity to rise above hesitation and claim the success they deserve. This transformation is not merely an outcome; it is a way of life, one that empowers individuals to thrive in the face of challenges and embrace the full scope of their potential.

SETTING A FORWARD-LOOKING VISION

Overcoming doubt is not just about addressing the present but also about envisioning a future unshackled by its constraints. A forward-looking vision provides a powerful antidote to the self-limiting beliefs that doubt often fosters. It involves crafting a mental picture of success—not necessarily defined by conventional metrics like promotions or titles but by personal fulfillment, meaningful contributions, and alignment with one's values. This vision acts as a guiding star, offering clarity and direction amid uncertainty and hesitation.

To create such a vision, individuals must first confront the narratives that doubt perpetuates. These narratives, often internalized over years, frame the future as a place of risk rather than opportunity. Rewriting these scripts begins with an honest appraisal of one's strengths and aspirations, coupled with a willingness to redefine what success looks like. This process is deeply personal, requiring individuals to ask hard questions: What truly matters to me? What kind of impact do I want to have? Answering these questions provides the foundation for a vision that feels authentic and motivating.

A forward-looking vision also requires setting clear, actionable goals that bridge the gap between where one is and where one aims to be. These goals must be specific and realistic, offering incremental steps toward the larger vision. For example, someone struggling with self-mistrust might set an initial goal of speaking up in meetings, gradually building the confidence to lead discussions. The act of setting and achieving these goals reinforces self-belief, creating a positive feedback loop that propels individuals closer to their envisioned future.

Equally important is the mindset with which this vision is approached. A forward-looking vision is not a rigid plan but a flexible framework, one that adapts to life's inevitable twists and turns. It acknowledges that setbacks are part of growth and that progress is often uneven. This flexibility allows individuals to remain resilient, focusing on the broader trajectory rather than getting discouraged by temporary obstacles. It also cultivates a sense of hope, which is crucial for maintaining momentum in the face of challenges.

Setting a forward-looking vision is about reclaiming agency. It shifts the focus from external validation to internal fulfillment, encouraging individuals to pursue paths that resonate with their authentic selves. This vision transforms insecurity from a barrier into a stepping stone, empowering individuals to not only overcome their fears but to actively shape a future that aligns with their deepest aspirations. By looking forward, individuals open themselves to the possibility of growth, success, and the profound satisfaction of living a life guided by purpose rather than fear.

Chapter 1: The Roots of Workplace Insecurity

Maria sat silently in the conference room, her palms sweating as she clutched her pen. The team was brainstorming ideas for an upcoming project, and Maria had a suggestion she was confident could work. But every time she considered speaking up, a voice in her head reminded her of the times her father had dismissed her ideas as impractical when she was growing up. "Better to stay quiet than to risk being wrong," she thought.

When her colleague James casually mentioned a concept similar to hers, the room erupted in approval. Maria smiled and nodded, hiding her frustration and shame behind a mask of agreement. It wasn't the first time she had held back in such moments, but each instance seemed to deepen the sense that she didn't belong, that she wasn't good enough.

Maria's hesitancy wasn't simply about fear of rejection—it was a reflection of years of internalized perfectionism and the subtle biases she had encountered throughout her career. While her upbringing instilled a fear of making mistakes, her experiences in a workplace dominated by louder, more assertive personalities reinforced her silence.

This cycle of insecurity, built on personal history and external challenges, is common yet often unrecognized. In Maria's case, it wasn't until she began to unpack the roots of her hesitations that she could begin to rebuild her confidence and change her professional trajectory.

PERSONAL HISTORY

Our earliest experiences often shape how we perceive ourselves and our place in the world, laying the groundwork for how we navigate professional environments. A critical or overly demanding upbringing, for example, can instill a deep-seated fear of failure. Children who grow up in environments where praise is rare and mistakes are magnified often internalize the belief that their worth depends on flawless performance. This mindset can carry over into adulthood, manifesting as perfectionism or an inability to take risks at work.

Similarly, education can play a significant role in fostering insecurity. In highly competitive academic settings, students are conditioned to measure their success against that of their peers. Grades, accolades, and other markers of achievement become proxies for self-worth. This relentless comparison doesn't disappear after graduation—it evolves into an obsession with metrics like promotions or performance reviews, perpetuating the cycle of indecisiveness in the workplace.

Societal pressures further compound these feelings. Cultural norms and expectations often dictate what success "should" look like, creating additional burdens. Women, for instance, might feel the need to overcompensate in male-dominated fields, while individuals from underrepresented backgrounds may struggle against stereotypes or implicit biases. These external expectations create an invisible script that many professionals feel compelled to follow, often at the cost of their own confidence.

Together, these elements of personal history—upbringing, education, and societal pressures—set the stage for insecurity to thrive. They shape how individuals approach challenges, interpret setbacks, and perceive their value within the professional sphere.

EXTERNAL FACTORS

While personal history lays the foundation for insecurity, external factors often act as amplifiers, reinforcing patterns of self-doubt in the workplace. Toxic environments, microaggressions, and implicit bias are among the most pervasive influences that erode confidence and hinder professional growth.

A toxic workplace, marked by favoritism, poor communication, or unrealistic demands, can make even the most competent employees question their abilities. When employees face criticism without constructive feedback or are consistently excluded from important conversations, they may begin to internalize these experiences as a reflection of their inadequacy. Over time, this environment fosters self-questioning and a reluctance to take initiative, trapping individuals in a cycle of insecurity.

Microaggressions—subtle, often unintentional, acts of bias—further exacerbate these feelings. For example, a manager who habitually interrupts women in meetings or overlooks contributions from minority employees may not realize the impact of their behavior. Yet, for the recipients, these repeated slights send a clear message: "Your voice matters less." Such experiences not only undermine confidence but also create barriers to trust and collaboration in the workplace.

Implicit bias adds another layer of complexity. These unconscious prejudices affect decision-making processes, such as hiring, promotions, and project assignments. Professionals from marginalized groups may find themselves working harder for the same recognition or opportunities as their peers, leading to burnout and a persistent sense of being undervalued. Even those who succeed often carry the weight of proving they belong, a burden that saps energy and fosters insecurity.

External factors like these don't just challenge individuals—they perpetuate systemic issues that keep workplaces from becoming inclusive and empowering environments. Understanding and addressing these influences is essential for anyone seeking to rebuild their confidence and thrive professionally.

IMPACT ON PROFESSIONAL INSECURITY

The interplay between personal history and external factors creates a fertile ground for professional insecurity, manifesting in behaviors that hinder career growth and workplace satisfaction. Over time, the weight of unaddressed internal struggles and external challenges compounds, shaping how individuals perceive themselves and their capabilities in a professional setting.

One common result is **over-preparation**. Insecure employees may feel compelled to work harder and longer to prove their worth, often overcompensating for their perceived inadequacies. While this might initially appear as diligence, it frequently leads to burnout, as individuals constantly strive to meet unattainable standards. The fear of making even minor mistakes can paralyze decision-making and creativity, depriving them of opportunities to showcase innovation or leadership.

On the other end of the spectrum, insecurity can also cause hesitation or avoidance. Employees plagued by lack of assurance may shy away from taking risks, such as volunteering for a challenging project or speaking up in meetings. This reluctance often stems from a fear of judgment or failure, limiting their visibility and professional growth. Over time, this avoidance reinforces feelings of inadequacy, creating a self-fulfilling cycle.

Other manifestations include perfectionism, fear of feedback, and comparison traps. Perfectionists may delay tasks out of fear they won't meet unrealistic standards, while those who fear feedback may interpret constructive criticism as a confirmation of their incompetence. Insecure professionals are also prone to measuring their success against that of others, particularly in the age of social media and platforms like LinkedIn, which amplify curated images of success. This constant comparison fosters envy, self-doubt, and a distorted sense of personal achievement.

Ultimately, the impact of insecurity is multifaceted and deeply ingrained, affecting not only how individuals perform but also how they feel about their work and their place within the organization. Understanding these patterns is the first step toward breaking free from them, enabling professionals to regain confidence and take ownership of their careers.

ACTIONABLE REFLECTION

Reflecting on the roots of insecurity is an essential step in breaking free from its grip. Start by considering the messages you received growing up about success and failure. Were you encouraged to strive for excellence, or were your mistakes magnified and criticized? These early experiences often shape how we approach challenges in adulthood, particularly in the workplace. If your upbringing involved pressure to meet high standards, it may have fostered a fear of failure that persists in your professional life, causing you to avoid risks or overcompensate with perfectionism.

Next, think about your education and how it influenced your sense of self-worth. Were you constantly compared to others, either by teachers or peers? If success was measured by grades or accolades, you might have internalized a sense of inadequacy when those markers were not achieved. This environment often leads to a constant measuring of success against others, even in the workplace. Reflect on whether you feel compelled to prove yourself, especially in environments where competition is prevalent or recognition is scarce. This sense of needing to "measure up" can foster deep insecurity, particularly when you feel you are falling short.

Consider the external factors that might contribute to your insecurity in the workplace. Have you experienced a toxic work culture, where communication is poor, favoritism prevails, or feedback is often unconstructive? These environments can lead to feelings of inadequacy and erode confidence, as employees are left uncertain about their performance or standing within the organization. Reflect on whether you've ever been overlooked for a promotion or project, or faced microaggressions that subtly undermined your contributions. These small yet cumulative actions can have a lasting impact, reinforcing feelings of uncertainty and marginalization.

Use this reflection to create a plan for change. Write about a recent situation where you felt insecure at work, and explore what triggered those feelings. Was it a past experience, an external challenge, or a combination of both? Identify one small, actionable step you could take in the future to address those feelings—whether it's contributing an idea in a meeting, setting boundaries in a challenging environment, or seeking constructive feedback from a trusted colleague. By exploring the underlying causes of hesitation or uncertainty, you can begin to take deliberate actions to strengthen your confidence and redefine your professional narrative.

How Insecurity Manifests

Insecurity often operates quietly, shaping behaviors in ways that seem harmless—or even helpful—on the surface. Consider a marketing manager who spends days fine-tuning a presentation, adding data points and polishing slides to perfection. To her colleagues, she appears thorough and committed. Yet, beneath the surface, her meticulous approach stems not from confidence but from a fear of being seen as inadequate. She over-prepares, hoping to guard against criticism, but the toll on her time and energy leaves little room for creative thinking or strategic planning.

This pattern is not unique to one role or industry. Across professions, feelings of inadequacy manifest in subtle but pervasive ways, from hesitating to contribute ideas in a meeting to avoiding feedback on a project altogether. These behaviors, though rooted in self-preservation, can inadvertently limit growth and professional success.

The challenge lies in recognizing these habits for what they are: manifestations of self-doubt. Often, they masquerade as strengths—dedication, caution, or humility—making them difficult to identify and even harder to address. By understanding how insecurity influences actions, professionals can begin to break free from its hold, reclaiming energy and focus for meaningful work.

This section explores the most common ways insecurity manifests in the workplace. From over-preparation to perfectionism and the constant trap of comparison, these patterns reveal how insecurity subtly—and powerfully—impacts both individual potential and organizational success.

OVER-PREPARATION, HESITATION, AND AVOIDANCE

Insecurity in the workplace often takes the form of over-preparation, hesitation, or outright avoidance. These behaviors, while seemingly unrelated, are driven by the same underlying fear: the worry of being judged, failing, or exposing perceived inadequacies. Each manifests differently but shares the same core effect—limiting growth and draining emotional energy.

Over-preparation is one of the most common ways insecurity shows up, particularly among high-achieving professionals. It may involve spending excessive time on tasks to ensure every detail is perfect, double-checking work to the point of inefficiency, or preparing exhaustive contingencies for imagined scenarios. While this effort can sometimes lead to short-term success, it often comes at the cost of burnout and diminished productivity. For example, an employee who spends hours perfecting a routine email risks losing valuable time that could have been spent on strategic initiatives.

Hesitation is another hallmark of insecurity, often stemming from a fear of making the wrong decision or drawing attention to oneself. This hesitation might look like delaying the submission of a report, refraining from voicing an idea in a meeting, or declining opportunities that require stepping out of one's comfort zone. While hesitation is sometimes mistaken for caution, it often reflects a paralyzing fear of judgment, which can stall career advancement and create missed opportunities.

Avoidance, perhaps the most detrimental behavior, occurs when individuals sidestep challenges altogether to shield themselves from potential failure or criticism. It might mean declining leadership roles, evading difficult conversations, or neglecting tasks that require a public presentation of their work. Over time, avoidance erodes confidence even further, as the absence of engagement reinforces feelings of inadequacy.

These behaviors may feel like protective mechanisms, but their cumulative effect is limiting. Over-preparation, hesitation, and avoidance create cycles of self-doubt, making it increasingly difficult to take risks or embrace opportunities. Recognizing these patterns is the first step in breaking free from their grip and developing more empowering responses to insecurity.

COMMON BEHAVIORS: PERFECTIONISM, FEAR OF FEEDBACK, AND COMPARISON TRAPS

Insecurity frequently drives specific behaviors that feel productive or protective but ultimately hold professionals back. Among the most pervasive are perfectionism, Fear of feedback and the comparison trap. Each reflects a distinct way of coping with insecurity, yet all share the capacity to undermine confidence and hinder growth.

Perfectionism often stems from a belief that only flawless performance will earn respect or acceptance. While the pursuit of high standards can be admirable, perfectionism takes this drive to an extreme, leaving little room for error or imperfection. A perfectionist might agonize over minor details of a project, delaying its completion for fear it won't meet their impossibly high standards. This behavior not only consumes valuable time but also fosters anxiety and inhibits learning, as the fear of failure outweighs the opportunity to improve through experience. The pressure to be perfect often leaves individuals feeling trapped in a cycle of inadequacy, no matter how much they achieve.

Fear of feedback is another common manifestation of insecurity, often rooted in the fear that constructive criticism will confirm one's perceived inadequacies. This fear can lead to avoiding performance reviews, downplaying the need for input, or reacting defensively to suggestions. While feedback is a critical tool for professional development, the insecure mind interprets it as a threat rather than an opportunity. Over time, this avoidance creates a barrier to growth, as the absence of constructive insights limits the chance to identify areas for improvement or build new skills.

The comparison trap, especially prevalent in today's social-media-driven world, feeds on insecurity by amplifying feelings of inadequacy. Professionals frequently measure their success against the curated lives of their peers, whether it's LinkedIn updates about promotions, awards, or other achievements. This endless cycle of comparison distorts reality, as people see only the highlights of others' careers while focusing on the flaws in their own. Such comparisons sap motivation and foster envy, leaving individuals feeling stuck and unworthy despite their accomplishments.

Perfectionism, fear of feedback, and the comparison trap all serve as barriers to confidence and success. They create environments where individuals feel constantly judged—by themselves and others—resulting in missed opportunities for growth and connection. Recognizing these behaviors and understanding their roots is crucial to dismantling them, freeing professionals to focus on progress over perfection, learning over fear, and personal growth over external validation.

THE COST OF THESE BEHAVIORS

The behaviors driven by insecurity—over-preparation, hesitation, avoidance, perfectionism, fear of feedback, and falling into the comparison trap—come at a significant cost, both professionally and personally. While they may seem like protective mechanisms or efforts to excel, their long-term effects often undermine the very success and fulfillment individuals seek.

In the workplace, these behaviors can diminish productivity and performance. Over-preparation, for instance, consumes excessive time and energy, leading to missed deadlines or an inability to prioritize tasks effectively. Hesitation delays decision-making and stifles innovation, as professionals may hold back ideas or fail to seize opportunities that could advance their careers. Avoidance further compounds the issue by keeping individuals from tackling challenges, taking on leadership roles, or engaging in the kind of visibility necessary for growth. Each behavior creates a self-reinforcing loop of missed opportunities and heightened insecurity.

The personal toll is just as profound. Perfectionism, while often seen as a badge of honor, leads to chronic stress and burnout as individuals push themselves to unattainable standards. Fear of feedback can isolate professionals, making them feel disconnected from colleagues and depriving them of valuable support and insights. The comparison trap, fueled by social media and workplace competition, fosters feelings of inadequacy and resentment, eroding self-esteem and creating a constant sense of dissatisfaction with one's achievements.

Over time, these behaviors can shape a narrative of limitation, where individuals begin to see themselves as incapable or unworthy of success. This not only affects their confidence but also their ability to build meaningful professional relationships, as insecurity often manifests as defensiveness, withdrawal, or overcompensation. Teams and organizations also suffer when talented individuals hold back, depriving the group of fresh perspectives and ideas.

The cost of these behaviors extends beyond immediate circumstances, influencing career trajectories and personal well-being in profound ways. Recognizing and addressing these patterns is essential for breaking free from the cycle of self-limiting beliefs and unlocking one's full potential. By understanding the price of actions driven by fear of failure, individuals can take the first step toward reclaiming their confidence and charting a path toward growth and fulfillment.

REFLECTION AND NEXT STEPS

Reflecting on the ways insecurity manifests is an opportunity to gain clarity and start taking steps toward meaningful change. Begin by asking yourself how these behaviors have shown up in your own professional life. Have you ever spent countless hours refining a task, not because it demanded perfection, but because you feared it wouldn't be good enough? Or perhaps you've avoided opportunities or feedback out of fear of being exposed or criticized. Acknowledging these moments is not about self-judgment but about creating awareness.

Think about the impact of these behaviors on your career and well-being. What have you sacrificed in terms of time, energy, or missed opportunities? Maybe you hesitated to apply for a role you wanted, or you passed up the chance to speak in a meeting where your insights could have made a difference. Consider how these actions, rooted in insecurity, may have reinforced feelings of inadequacy over time. This process of reflection is essential for understanding the cost of inaction and the potential rewards of change.

Next, identify a specific pattern you want to address and commit to one small but meaningful step forward. For example, if over-preparation is a recurring issue, challenge yourself to set a firm time limit for completing your next task and stick to it. If fear of feedback holds you back, take the initiative to seek input from a trusted colleague, framing it as an opportunity for growth. Small, consistent actions like these not only disrupt unhelpful patterns but also build confidence over time.

Remind yourself that these behaviors are not fixed traits but patterns shaped by past experiences and external pressures—patterns that can be reshaped.

Approach this journey with patience and self-compassion, recognizing that each step toward addressing these challenges brings you closer to personal and professional empowerment. Change begins with awareness, but true transformation arises from the courage to take action despite uncertainty. Every effort you make to confront these barriers is an investment in your growth and potential.

Chapter 2: Confidence in New Roles

Change begins with awareness, but true transformation comes from the courage to act in spite of uncertainty. Every step you take to confront insecurity is an investment in your growth and potential. While often dismissed as just "first-day jitters," impostor syndrome can run much deeper, impacting confidence and overall performance. Impostor syndrome in new roles is particularly challenging because the unfamiliarity of the workplace, combined with high expectations and the pressure to prove oneself, can amplify insecurities. People experiencing this doubt often feel as though they don't belong or fear being "exposed" as underqualified despite their achievements. Rather than signaling true inadequacy, these feelings typically reflect an inner tension as one adjusts to a new environment.

Understanding the nature of imposter syndrome is crucial to addressing it effectively. It is marked by feelings of inadequacy, insecurity, and a constant fear that any success achieved is undeserved. Unlike typical nerves, impostor syndrome involves a pervasive sense that one's accomplishments are the result of luck or deception, rather than genuine skill or merit. In new roles, this mindset can be overwhelming, especially when coupled with a steep learning curve or the challenge of adapting to an established team. It's essential to recognize that these feelings, though intense, are rooted in perception rather than fact. Acknowledging impostor syndrome for what it is—a set of feelings rather than a reflection of competence—can be the first step in managing it.

The triggers for impostor syndrome in new job roles often stem from a heightened awareness of being evaluated. On the first day, most people strive to create a positive impression, but this natural desire can backfire, making them hypercritical of their actions and performance. Starting a job with expectations from others, or even self-imposed ideals of success, can lead to an intense focus on perceived shortcomings. Additionally, there's the issue of comparison: in established teams, new hires may feel pressure to "catch up" to colleagues' familiarity and competence. By understanding these triggers, individuals can begin to disentangle valid, situational challenges from the irrational doubts that impostor syndrome often brings.

One of the most empowering realizations about impostor syndrome is its universality. Many accomplished professionals—from CEOs to award-winning artists—have admitted to feeling like frauds at some point in their careers, especially when starting something new. Recognizing that impostor syndrome is common can help reframe it as a natural, temporary part of growth rather than a debilitating flaw. This perspective not only normalizes the experience but can also inspire those dealing with it to embrace rather than fear it. Instead of letting impostor syndrome hold them back, new hires can view it as a stepping stone in their journey to greater self-confidence and professional success.

STRATEGIES FOR OVERCOMING IMPOSTOR SYNDROME

When beginning a new role, overcoming impostor syndrome requires a combination of self-awareness and intentional actions that help shift one's mindset. Recognizing impostor syndrome as a natural response to unfamiliar situations can be reassuring; however, developing a strategy to address it is key to building resilience and self-assurance. One of the most effective ways to combat impostor syndrome is to reframe the way we think about challenges in the workplace. Instead of seeing new tasks or responsibilities as tests of inherent ability, it can help to view them as opportunities to learn and grow. Shifting from a focus on "proving" oneself to simply progressing in the role can alleviate the stress that impostor syndrome often brings. This approach not only reduces pressure but also encourages a healthier, more sustainable outlook on career development.

In addition to reframing challenges, cultivating positive self-talk and visualization can be powerful tools for managing uncertainty. For instance, replacing negative thoughts with constructive affirmations—such as reminding oneself of their preparedness, skillset, and achievements—helps in building a more balanced self-image. Visualization techniques, where individuals imagine themselves succeeding in a task or interaction, can also ease anxiety by making new experiences feel familiar. This mental rehearsal is beneficial because it prepares the mind for confidence and minimizes the element of surprise that can trigger insecurity. Both positive self-talk and visualization require practice, but over time, they contribute to a mindset that sees the new job as an opportunity rather than a challenge to one's competence.

Limiting comparisons with colleagues is another crucial strategy in overcoming impostor syndrome, as constant comparison tends to amplify self-doubt. It's easy to look at team members who seem confident and competent and to feel inadequate by comparison. However, every professional has a unique journey, and comparing oneself to others can distort one's perception of their own growth. Focusing on individual goals and achievements can help new hires appreciate their unique contributions rather than feeling overshadowed. Setting personal goals—small, achievable milestones within the new role—can keep attention on personal growth rather than perceived shortcomings. This approach fosters a sense of progress and accomplishment that is rooted in one's own effort, not external validation.

Developing self-assurance also involves recognizing and celebrating small successes, which are often overlooked when struggling with impostor syndrome. While it's common to focus on bigger achievements, acknowledging minor victories, such as completing a challenging task or receiving positive feedback, reinforces a positive self-image. Keeping a log of these accomplishments—whether through journaling or an online document—can serve as a reminder of progress and resilience during moments of doubt. This record becomes a personal confidence booster, showing evidence of growth and capability that is useful to revisit during challenging times. Each of these strategies, when practiced consistently, helps build a foundation of confidence, allowing new hires to approach their roles with a greater sense of self-worth and competence.

BUILDING CONFIDENCE THROUGH PREPARATION AND EARLY WINS

Confidence in a new role often begins with a strong foundation of preparation. Taking time before the first day to research the company's mission, values, and goals can foster a sense of familiarity and alignment with the organization's purpose, helping new hires feel less like outsiders and more like contributors from the start. Learning about team structures, recent projects, and even a bit about the key individuals one will be working with can provide valuable context. When new hires understand the bigger picture, they gain confidence in their place within it, seeing how their unique skills and experiences can benefit the team. Preparation doesn't remove all uncertainty, but it does equip individuals with the knowledge and mindset to engage more fully, feel grounded in their role, and respond confidently to the unexpected.

Preparation should extend beyond understanding the company's landscape and encompass specific role-related skills and knowledge. Reviewing relevant processes, studying tools and systems, or even refreshing industry knowledge can bolster readiness. For instance, if the new job requires learning a particular software, familiarizing oneself with its basics beforehand can turn a daunting task into a manageable one. Likewise, engaging with industry trends can foster confidence by reinforcing the idea that one is not only prepared but also proactive. This readiness allows new hires to start with a sense of empowerment, showing both themselves and their team that they are prepared to add value. Preparation thus becomes a visible indicator of commitment, and each moment of prior knowledge realized in real-time interactions reinforces the new hire's sense of belonging and competence.

Once in the role, achieving early wins is crucial for solidifying confidence. These small successes can create a positive feedback loop, encouraging a productive mindset and helping individuals gain momentum. Early wins might include completing a minor project, contributing useful insights in meetings, or building rapport with a key team member. Such achievements, though modest in scope, serve as proof of one's capability and offer a reassuring contrast to the insecurity that often accompanies imposter syndrome. Each small success builds a foundation of confidence, helping new hires see their own potential and capability in action. Early wins serve as mental markers that affirm their skills, ease performance anxiety, and counterbalance fears of inadequacy.

Building a support network within the new environment further reinforces early successes. Reaching out to colleagues for insights, advice, or simply to establish rapport can create an invaluable resource for the initial transition period. A few positive relationships can make the new environment feel more supportive and collaborative, as well as offer direct guidance when facing uncertainty. Seeking feedback from these trusted colleagues can also provide constructive perspectives and highlight strengths that the new hire may overlook. As these connections grow, they serve not only as a professional network but as a reminder of one's place and value within the organization. This sense of belonging—amplified through preparation, early achievements, and supportive relationships—builds a resilient confidence that transforms the new role from a potential source of anxiety into a meaningful opportunity for growth.

Making an Impression

In any new role, the temptation to present a polished, idealized version of oneself can be strong. Many people believe that impressing colleagues and managers requires a flawless display of professionalism, knowledge, and confidence. However, the reality is that authentic connections are built through genuine, honest interactions rather than through perfection. Embracing authenticity means allowing one's true personality and unique strengths to shine through, rather than striving to meet a preconceived notion of what success looks like. By doing so, new hires create a foundation of trust and openness, inviting others to engage with them sincerely. Colleagues and managers are often more receptive to someone who is authentic, as it demonstrates both confidence and integrity—qualities that build credibility over time.

Authenticity in the workplace doesn't mean revealing every personal detail or downplaying one's professional demeanor; it's about conveying a true sense of who one is. This can include sharing genuine interests, acknowledging areas for growth, and recognizing the contributions of others. For example, if a new hire isn't familiar with a particular process or tool, openly asking for guidance not only shows humility but also fosters an environment where colleagues feel valued as mentors. Such transparency can encourage mutual respect and open communication, creating a positive feedback loop of trust. Colleagues who see that a new team member is sincere are more likely to offer support and see that person as someone they want to work with closely. This authenticity establishes a foundation upon which deeper, more meaningful connections can develop.

Attempting to project an idealized persona can often backfire, leading to unnecessary stress and detachment. When people suppress their natural behaviors or adopt a highly curated version of themselves, interactions may feel strained, and colleagues may sense a lack of sincerity. Authenticity, on the other hand, is naturally attractive—it invites others to connect on a human level, creating an atmosphere of openness and approachability. By being genuine, new hires signal to others that they are not just "filling a role" but are present as real, multifaceted individuals, willing to contribute and grow. Authenticity can also defuse tension in challenging situations, as it allows individuals to address issues openly rather than avoiding them or masking uncertainty. This helps cultivate a work culture of empathy and shared understanding, where colleagues can engage more openly and supportively.

In today's workplace, where collaboration and interpersonal skills are highly valued, authenticity has become a key component of professional success. Managers and colleagues often respond better to individuals who display their genuine selves, rather than those who present a front that might appear overly rehearsed or guarded. New hires who commit to an authentic approach in their early days are setting the tone for their work relationships, demonstrating a confidence that comes from embracing one's true character rather than a fabricated image. The willingness to be oneself, even in moments of vulnerability, reflects a level of self-assurance that colleagues and managers respect and admire. By starting with authenticity, new employees don't just make an impression; they lay the groundwork for trust, collaboration, and meaningful relationships that will serve them well throughout their career journey.

ACTIVE LISTENING AND ADAPTABILITY AS TOOLS FOR BUILDING RAPPORT

Building rapport in a new workplace environment requires more than making a good first impression; it involves fostering genuine connections by understanding and responding to the perspectives of others. Active listening is one of the most powerful tools for achieving this. When we actively listen, we demonstrate respect and a willingness to understand our colleagues' viewpoints. Rather than focusing on formulating responses, active listening requires being fully present, absorbing both verbal and nonverbal cues. This approach not only helps us grasp the explicit details of what others say but also allows us to sense underlying concerns, motivations, and values. In a new role, where team dynamics are still unfamiliar, the practice of active listening can be instrumental in quickly building rapport, as colleagues feel genuinely valued and understood.

The benefits of active listening extend beyond simply gathering information; it is a bridge to understanding workplace culture and norms. New hires are often faced with an array of unspoken rules, team values, and individual personalities that can't be learned from a job description. By listening attentively, new employees can absorb these nuances, observing how their colleagues interact, approach tasks, and solve problems. This deeper awareness enables them to adapt their own behavior in ways that align with the team's needs and expectations. For instance, they may notice that certain colleagues prefer detailed discussions, while others favor quick, decisive actions. By recognizing and responding to these preferences, new hires can tailor their communication styles accordingly, fostering smoother interactions and reducing misunderstandings. This adaptability signals to colleagues that the new team member respects their way of working, which is essential for building trust and credibility.

Adaptability complements active listening by allowing new hires to apply what they learn in real time. In the early stages of a new role, flexibility is crucial, as it demonstrates a willingness to contribute to the team's goals rather than focusing solely on personal routines or preferences. Colleagues are more likely to respond positively to a new team member who shows openness to changing plans, adopting new methods, or rethinking assumptions based on the feedback they receive. Adaptability in this context goes beyond simply adjusting one's approach; it reflects a proactive commitment to mutual success. This willingness to evolve not only strengthens relationships but also establishes a reputation for resilience and versatility, traits that are highly valued in most modern work environments.

Together, active listening and adaptability form a powerful foundation for building lasting rapport. They work in tandem: active listening provides insight, while adaptability turns that insight into effective action. Colleagues who feel that their perspectives are understood and that their work preferences are respected will view the new hire as someone who values collaboration and harmony. Over time, these positive interactions compound, creating an environment where trust and respect naturally develop. A new employee who masters these skills is not only more likely to succeed in their role but will also lay the groundwork for meaningful, productive relationships that support both individual and team goals. In a workplace landscape that increasingly values emotional intelligence and cooperation, the ability to listen and adapt is more than a tool for success—it's a hallmark of a true professional.

DEMONSTRATING RELIABILITY THROUGH CONSISTENT ACTION

Reliability is one of the most valued qualities in any workplace, and in a new role, it can be a powerful way to build credibility and trust. Demonstrating reliability starts with consistently following through on commitments, however small they may seem. When a new hire reliably completes tasks on time, delivers work to expected standards, and maintains clear communication, it sends a message to colleagues and managers: this is someone who can be counted on. In the first few weeks, these initial actions help establish a reputation. Unlike grand gestures or big projects, reliability is built through the steady fulfillment of everyday responsibilities, creating a strong foundation for one's professional image. As these actions accumulate, they foster a sense of trust and stability that's essential for building rapport with a team.

The impact of reliability becomes especially significant in collaborative environments, where the success of one person often depends on the timely contributions of others. When a new team member consistently meets deadlines and communicates effectively, they reduce uncertainty for their colleagues, allowing the team to work more efficiently. This consistency helps alleviate any anxieties colleagues might have about working with someone new. Reliability, in this sense, is about respecting others' time and workloads by ensuring that one's contributions support the collective effort rather than disrupting it. In the early stages of a role, when coworkers are still assessing whether they can trust the new hire, reliability offers a clear and measurable sign that they're a valuable, dependable part of the team.

Consistency in action also provides new employees with an opportunity to demonstrate their professionalism and commitment to quality. Each completed task, no matter how minor, serves as a tangible example of their work ethic and attention to detail. This focus on delivering consistent, quality work helps to cultivate a reputation for integrity. For example, if a new hire volunteers to take on a small task in a team project, completing it with care and timeliness reinforces that they take all responsibilities seriously. These actions reflect a dedication to the role that goes beyond just fulfilling job requirements; they show a commitment to excellence that colleagues and managers can recognize and appreciate. Over time, this steady output of reliable work builds a strong professional identity, setting the stage for future opportunities and greater responsibilities within the team.

Reliability, however, is not only about completing tasks but also about communicating proactively when challenges arise. Situations may not always go as planned, and unexpected setbacks are common in any work environment. When difficulties emerge, reliable employees maintain their credibility by informing colleagues or supervisors in a timely manner, adjusting timelines, or seeking help if needed. This approach demonstrates accountability and shows that they are willing to take responsibility rather than allowing others to be surprised by missed deadlines or incomplete tasks. This transparency strengthens trust, as it shows that the new team member values the success of the team above personal pride. By balancing consistent action with honest communication, new hires solidify their reputation as reliable contributors who prioritize the team's success.

Reliability is a quality that builds gradually but pays significant dividends. For new hires, demonstrating this quality can help integrate them into a team more quickly, establish a positive professional identity, and foster long-term relationships based on mutual respect. By proving themselves through consistent actions, they are effectively saying, "You can trust me to be a reliable part of this team." This trust, once established, becomes a foundation upon which future collaboration, support, and growth are built, allowing them to navigate the challenges of a new role with the confidence that their team stands behind them.

Chapter 3: Thriving Through Transitions

Adapting to change, especially in a professional context, can be a deeply unsettling experience. The fear of stepping into the unknown, the anxiety of being perceived as inexperienced, and the pressure to prove oneself often converge to create a heightened state of stress. This emotional upheaval isn't just an isolated incident but rather a natural, almost primal response. Human beings are wired to seek comfort and predictability; this desire for stability is embedded in our psychology, an evolutionary trait meant to ensure survival. When faced with change, especially in the workplace where we spend a significant portion of our lives, it triggers a threat response. This reaction is tied to our limbic system, the part of the brain responsible for emotions and survival instincts. The unknown feels dangerous, and as a result, we become hyper-vigilant, scrutinizing our surroundings and doubting our capabilities. The psychological impact of change is thus not just about the new environment or the new role—it's about confronting our own deep-seated fears and insecurities.

Moreover, change often acts as a mirror, reflecting back to us aspects of our self-perception that we might not usually confront. For many professionals, the discomfort of a new job or a shift in industry forces them to question their value and relevance. Questions like "Am I capable of succeeding here?" or "Will others see me as competent?" start to bubble up, often subconsciously, eroding self-confidence. This erosion can be particularly challenging for individuals who have already struggled with self-doubt or have experienced imposter syndrome in the past. The new context feels like a fresh stage where the spotlight is on them, highlighting every perceived flaw or knowledge gap. This magnification of self-criticism is a common psychological response during transitions, as the brain naturally focuses on potential threats rather than opportunities. It's not just the unfamiliar tasks or unknown colleagues that cause stress—it's the internal dialogue, the stories we tell ourselves about our own worth and capability, that often present the biggest barrier.

This heightened sense of vulnerability during transitions is also tied to the concept of social identity. In the workplace, our roles and positions often become intertwined with our sense of self. When a change disrupts this, it can feel as though a piece of our identity is being challenged or taken away. Imagine a professional who has spent years establishing themselves as an expert in a particular field, only to suddenly find themselves in a completely different industry. The skills and knowledge they once relied on to define their success may now feel irrelevant or insufficient. This dissonance between who they were in their previous role and who they need to become in the new context can create an intense psychological strain. It's as though they are standing on shifting ground, trying to regain their balance while simultaneously adjusting to new expectations and learning the unspoken rules of a different culture. This struggle with identity can make the process of adaptation seem not just difficult but fundamentally disorienting.

Furthermore, the emotional responses that arise during such transitions are often compounded by societal and cultural pressures. In many professional environments, there is an unspoken expectation that we should be adaptable and resilient, that change is an opportunity to showcase our flexibility and growth mindset. While this perspective can be empowering for some, it can also create an additional layer of pressure for those who are already feeling uncertain. The fear of appearing weak or unprepared can lead individuals to mask their anxiety, pushing themselves to project confidence even when they feel anything but confident inside. This performative aspect of dealing with change can intensify the psychological toll, as it creates a disconnect between how we feel and how we believe we are expected to appear. It's a cycle of insecurity reinforced by the fear of external judgment, making the process of adaptation even more draining. The psychological impact of change, therefore, goes beyond the surface-level challenges of learning new skills or adjusting to a new role; it delves into deeper issues of self-perception, identity, and the societal narratives we internalize about what it means to be successful in times of transition.

DEVELOPING A STRATEGIC MINDSET FOR CHANGE

Navigating change successfully requires more than just adapting to new circumstances; it necessitates a fundamental shift in mindset. A strategic mindset is one that embraces change not as a disruption to be feared, but as a valuable opportunity for growth and transformation. This approach involves cultivating a forward-thinking perspective, where the emphasis is on understanding the broader implications of the transition and how it fits into one's long-term career vision. When faced with a new job, industry shift, or unfamiliar environment, individuals with a strategic mindset focus on the possibilities that lie ahead rather than the potential pitfalls. They consciously frame change as a gateway to new experiences, skills, and connections, effectively reorienting their initial anxiety into productive curiosity. This mindset isn't about blind optimism; it's about deliberately choosing to view change as a series of challenges that, when met with preparation and intentional action, can be transformed into stepping stones for future success.

One of the key elements of developing a strategic mindset during transitions is the ability to set clear, realistic objectives. Change can often feel overwhelming because it presents a multitude of unknowns all at once. Professionals who are strategic take the time to break down the transition into manageable goals, focusing on incremental progress rather than immediate mastery. For instance, when starting in a new role, rather than aiming to prove expertise right away, a strategic approach would prioritize understanding the organizational culture, building rapport with key stakeholders, and identifying initial quick wins that can establish credibility. This type of structured, goal-oriented thinking not only reduces the chaos associated with change but also provides a roadmap that aligns actions with desired outcomes. It allows individuals to navigate transitions with purpose, maintaining a sense of control and direction even in uncertain environments. By setting short-term, achievable goals, professionals can experience early successes that build confidence and momentum, reinforcing their strategic approach to the larger transition process.

A crucial component of this mindset is also the willingness to engage in continuous learning. Change inherently involves venturing into unknown territory, and a strategic mindset embraces this as an opportunity for skill enhancement and knowledge acquisition. Instead of viewing gaps in understanding as failures or shortcomings, individuals who adopt a strategic perspective see them as areas ripe for growth. They proactively seek out resources, whether it's enrolling in a relevant course, seeking mentorship, or dedicating time to self-study, to fill those gaps. This approach not only helps bridge the knowledge divide but also demonstrates adaptability and a commitment to self-improvement—qualities that are highly valued in any professional setting. The emphasis is placed on the process of learning rather than on immediate perfection, which alleviates some of the pressure and insecurity that often accompany transitions. By embracing the role of a learner, rather than solely that of an expert, individuals can navigate the complexities of change with greater resilience and flexibility.

Finally, developing a strategic mindset involves cultivating patience and long-term thinking. In the fast-paced nature of today's work environments, there is often an unspoken expectation to quickly demonstrate competence and fit. However, a strategic mindset understands that true adaptation takes time and that success in new roles or industries is a gradual process. Professionals who thrive through transitions are those who are willing to give themselves the necessary time to adjust and learn without succumbing to the pressure of immediate validation. They adopt a broader perspective, recognizing that the discomfort of change is temporary and that their efforts will compound over time, leading to greater rewards in the future. This kind of patience is not passive but rather an active choice to focus on sustainable progress rather than short-term gains. It involves trusting the process, even when the outcomes are not immediately visible, and maintaining a clear vision of the bigger picture. By committing to this patient, strategic approach, individuals can navigate change more effectively, positioning themselves for long-term career growth and fulfillment.

ACTIONABLE STRATEGIES FOR NAVIGATING JOB CHANGES

Navigating a job change effectively requires more than just updating your resume and showing up on the first day—it demands a set of proactive, actionable strategies that can help manage the challenges and uncertainties of the transition. The first and most crucial step is conducting a thorough self-assessment before diving into the new role. This involves reflecting on your strengths, skills, and experiences, and how they align with the expectations of the new position. By identifying where you feel confident and where there may be gaps, you can create a tailored plan to address these areas proactively. For example, if you recognize that a new job requires familiarity with a specific software or industry knowledge you currently lack, taking a brief online course or reaching out to a mentor for insights can help bridge this gap before it becomes a stumbling block. Self-assessment is not about dwelling on deficiencies but about empowering yourself with a clear understanding of where you stand and what you can do to excel from the start. It sets the stage for a smoother transition by giving you a sense of direction and control, reducing the anxiety that often accompanies job changes.

Another essential strategy is to prioritize relationship-building from the very beginning. One of the biggest hurdles in adapting to a new role is integrating into the existing social fabric of the workplace. Often, we focus solely on the technical or task-related aspects of a job change, neglecting the significant impact that interpersonal dynamics can have on our success. Building rapport with your new colleagues, managers, and stakeholders should be a top priority in the initial weeks. This doesn't mean forcing connections or engaging in superficial networking but rather taking the time to understand the team's culture, communication styles, and unspoken norms. A strategic approach involves setting up brief one-on-one meetings with key individuals to introduce yourself, learn about their roles, and seek their advice or perspective on how to succeed in your new position. Such efforts demonstrate your willingness to integrate and learn, while also establishing a foundation of trust and goodwill. By actively cultivating these relationships early on, you create a supportive network that can provide guidance, feedback, and opportunities as you navigate your new environment.

In addition to building relationships, it's important to establish quick wins early in the transition process. Quick wins are small, achievable goals that showcase your competence and help build your credibility within the organization. These could be completing a project ahead of schedule, streamlining a minor process, or providing a fresh perspective in a team meeting. The objective is not to take on significant, high-risk tasks immediately but to identify areas where you can make a positive impact with relative ease. By delivering these early successes, you signal to your colleagues and superiors that you are capable and resourceful, which can help alleviate any doubts they may have about your fit for the role. This approach also serves as a confidence booster for you, reinforcing your sense of capability in the new job. It creates a momentum that can carry you through more challenging tasks and projects as you continue to acclimate to the new responsibilities. The key is to look for opportunities that align with your existing strengths and expertise while also contributing to the team's immediate needs.

It's crucial to practice adaptability and remain open to feedback during the initial stages of a job change. Even with extensive preparation and strong efforts, there will inevitably be aspects of the new role that don't go as planned or feel unfamiliar. Being adaptable means approaching these situations with a mindset of learning rather than frustration. Instead of feeling discouraged by constructive criticism, view it as a valuable source of information about the expectations and standards of your new workplace. Make it a habit to regularly check in with your manager or peers for informal feedback, asking questions like, "What can I do to better support our goals?" or "Is there anything I could improve on from the past project?" This openness not only demonstrates your commitment to growth but also shows that you are receptive and willing to make adjustments. By actively seeking out and integrating feedback, you can more quickly align your efforts with the team's objectives and establish yourself as a responsive and capable team member. This strategy, coupled with ongoing self-reflection, relationship-building, and the pursuit of quick wins, forms a comprehensive approach to navigating job changes with confidence and resilience.

BUILDING A SUPPORT NETWORK DURING TRANSITIONS

Transitions in a professional context, especially those involving job changes, can often feel like stepping into uncharted territory. It's during these periods of uncertainty that the need for a solid support network becomes most apparent. Building this network, however, isn't simply about having a few contacts in your industry or a couple of friends at work; it's about deliberately cultivating relationships that can provide guidance, insight, and emotional support when navigating the complexities of a new role. The first layer of this network often includes mentors—those who have already walked the path you are now embarking on. Reaching out to a mentor as you transition into a new job can provide invaluable insights, from understanding company culture to mastering specific role expectations. Instead of waiting for problems to arise, proactively seeking mentorship allows you to gain foresight and avoid common pitfalls. A mentor can offer perspective on how to handle difficult situations and help you strategize for success, reducing the anxiety that typically accompanies new challenges.

Equally important is connecting with your peers and colleagues within the organization. While mentorship offers a top-down perspective, the camaraderie of colleagues provides a horizontal form of support that is equally vital. These are the individuals who share your level of experience and are often dealing with similar challenges. Building rapport with your immediate team members fosters a sense of belonging and makes the transition process less isolating. Simple acts like inviting a coworker for coffee, engaging in small talk, or joining team activities can go a long way in creating a positive rapport. By showing genuine interest in your peers' experiences and contributions, you not only build connections but also create allies who can offer practical help and advice as you adapt to your new role. Additionally, having peers you can trust makes it easier to ask for clarification or assistance when you encounter unfamiliar processes or expectations, which can significantly speed up your acclimation period.

Beyond the workplace, tapping into broader professional networks can also be a strategic move during transitions. Industry associations, alumni groups, and online professional communities are excellent resources for expanding your support system beyond your immediate work environment. These networks can be especially helpful if you are changing industries or moving into a role that is vastly different from your previous experience. By participating in webinars, attending industry conferences, or joining online discussions relevant to your new position, you expose yourself to a wealth of shared knowledge and experiences. Engaging with a broader community allows you to ask questions, gather advice, and even discover potential resources or tools that you might not have been aware of otherwise. Moreover, the external perspective gained from these broader networks can provide valuable context and help you see beyond the specific culture of your new workplace, giving you a more balanced view of the challenges and opportunities that lie ahead.

Lastly, it is crucial to include a personal element in your support network. Friends, family, and loved ones play an essential role in providing the emotional backing that professional contacts might not be able to offer. They are the ones who see you beyond your job title and who can provide comfort and reassurance when the pressure of a new position feels overwhelming. However, it's important to communicate your needs effectively to them during this transition phase. Let them know what kind of support would be most helpful, whether it's giving you space to process your thoughts, offering a listening ear, or simply spending quality time away from work-related stress. Balancing professional and personal support ensures that you have a holistic safety net as you navigate the challenges of your new role. Together, these different layers of a support network—mentors, colleagues, broader professional contacts, and loved ones—create a robust foundation that can help you thrive during transitions. This comprehensive approach not only eases the immediate stress of adapting to change but also lays the groundwork for sustained success and growth in your new career path.

CASE STUDY: SUCCESS IN TRANSITION

To illustrate the importance and impact of strategic navigation during professional transitions, let's examine the real-life journey of Mia, a marketing professional who faced a daunting career shift. Mia had spent nearly a decade working in a well-established consumer goods company, where she excelled in traditional marketing roles. Her experience was rooted in well-defined brand campaigns, and she had developed a deep familiarity with the company's products, culture, and industry dynamics. However, as the digital landscape evolved, Mia recognized a need to expand her skill set and move toward digital marketing—a field she had limited experience in but which was rapidly becoming a critical component of her industry. Deciding to take a bold step, she applied for a role in a fast-growing tech startup, which would not only require her to pivot into digital marketing but also adapt to a vastly different organizational environment.

Upon starting her new job, Mia immediately encountered challenges that tested her adaptability and resilience. The startup's culture was worlds apart from the structured environment she was used to; it was dynamic, fast-paced, and required a level of agility she hadn't experienced before. Instead of predefined roles, the expectations were fluid, and Mia quickly realized that she was expected to take ownership of projects without the detailed guidelines she had been accustomed to. Initially, this threw her off balance. She found herself questioning her decision and struggling with imposter syndrome, doubting her ability to succeed in this unfamiliar terrain. However, rather than succumbing to these doubts, Mia decided to approach the transition strategically. She began by mapping out a personal plan for her first 90 days, setting small, achievable goals that focused on building her knowledge of digital tools, learning the company's processes, and understanding her new team's dynamics.

A crucial part of Mia's strategy was leveraging mentorship. Instead of relying solely on her own efforts, she reached out to a mentor she had met at an industry conference—a digital marketing specialist with extensive experience in the tech sector. This mentor provided her with valuable guidance on the nuances of digital marketing, shared key resources, and helped Mia identify the most critical skills she needed to focus on. The mentor's insights helped Mia prioritize her learning, allowing her to build competence in key areas without feeling overwhelmed by the breadth of new information. This relationship also gave Mia the confidence boost she needed, as her mentor's encouragement and reassurance helped counteract her imposter syndrome. By seeking mentorship, Mia was able to accelerate her learning curve significantly, positioning herself as a quick learner in her new role.

Simultaneously, Mia made a conscious effort to build a strong support network within her new workplace. Recognizing that her success depended not just on her technical skills but also on how well she integrated with her team, she focused on forming positive relationships early on. She scheduled informal one-on-one meetings with her new colleagues, taking the time to learn about their roles, experiences, and expectations. This not only helped her gain a better understanding of the company's culture and workflow but also created allies who were willing to offer help when she needed it. By showing genuine interest in her colleagues and openly acknowledging when she was unfamiliar with certain aspects of the digital space, Mia earned their respect and fostered a collaborative environment. Her willingness to be vulnerable about her learning process, combined with her proactive approach, helped her quickly build credibility and trust within the team.

Over the course of her first six months, Mia's strategic approach paid off. She successfully launched her first digital marketing campaign, which exceeded the company's performance expectations and demonstrated her growing expertise in the field. More importantly, her ability to navigate the transition with a combination of strategic planning, mentorship, and strong relationship-building set her apart as a leader who could adapt to change. The experience not only expanded her skill set but also boosted her confidence, proving to herself and her colleagues that she could thrive in a completely new domain. Mia's story exemplifies the power of embracing a growth mindset during career transitions and highlights how combining strategic thinking with the support of a strong network can turn potential setbacks into opportunities for remarkable success.

Through Mia's experience, we see a clear roadmap for anyone facing similar transitions: start with a clear plan, seek out mentors for guidance, prioritize relationship-building, and embrace the discomfort of the learning curve as an essential part of growth. Her journey underscores the importance of being both proactive and adaptable, showing that even in the face of significant change, it is possible to not only survive but excel when equipped with the right mindset and strategies.

KEY TAKEAWAYS AND REFLECTIVE EXERCISE

In reflecting on the lessons drawn from navigating significant career transitions, there are several key takeaways that can help professionals not only manage but also thrive during periods of change. The first and perhaps most critical lesson is the importance of embracing a proactive approach. Career transitions, whether voluntary or imposed by circumstances, often bring uncertainty and discomfort. However, by adopting a strategic mindset and viewing the transition as an opportunity rather than a setback, individuals can take control of their narrative. This proactive stance involves setting clear, manageable goals for the initial period in the new role, identifying immediate learning opportunities, and focusing on building early wins. Such an approach helps in counteracting feelings of doubt and gives a sense of purpose and direction amidst the unfamiliar. It's about shifting from a reactive posture, where one is overwhelmed by change, to a forward-looking strategy that lays the groundwork for growth.

Another vital takeaway is the transformative power of mentorship during career transitions. As illustrated in the previous case study, having a mentor can make an enormous difference in navigating unfamiliar territory. A mentor not only provides technical knowledge and industry-specific advice but also offers a sense of reassurance that is crucial during times of self-doubt. The objective guidance of a mentor can help in identifying skill gaps and prioritizing areas of development, which accelerates the adaptation process. Additionally, mentors often share their own experiences of overcoming similar challenges, which can serve as both a roadmap and a source of inspiration. The key for individuals in transition is to actively seek out and cultivate these relationships, recognizing the value they bring not just in terms of professional growth but also in building confidence and resilience. Mentorship becomes a cornerstone for reducing the isolation often felt during such periods and can serve as a critical support mechanism for overcoming uncertainty.

Equally important is the focus on relationship-building within the new organizational environment. Successfully integrating into a new workplace goes beyond mastering the technical aspects of the job; it requires a deep understanding of the company's culture and the formation of strong, supportive professional relationships. By taking the initiative to connect with new colleagues, asking questions, and showing genuine interest in their experiences, individuals can create a network of allies who can offer guidance and support. The process of relationship-building should not be seen as secondary or superficial; rather, it is a fundamental component of a successful transition. Cultivating positive workplace relationships helps in gaining early insights into the unspoken rules of the new environment, provides a sense of belonging, and establishes a foundation of trust that can facilitate collaboration. Those who prioritize building these connections often find themselves more integrated, respected, and able to navigate the complexities of the new role more effectively.

To help consolidate these insights and encourage individuals to apply them in their own professional journeys, it is useful to conclude with a reflective exercise. Take a moment to think about a transition you have experienced in your career—whether it was moving to a new company, changing industries, or taking on a significantly different role. Reflect on the following questions: How did you initially approach the transition? What strategies did you use to adapt, and were they effective? Did you seek guidance from a mentor or rely solely on your own efforts? How proactive were you in building relationships in your new environment, and what impact did that have on your experience? Finally, consider what you might do differently if faced with a similar transition in the future. These reflections are not merely about reviewing past actions but about identifying patterns, learning from previous experiences, and applying those insights to future career challenges. By consciously engaging in this reflection, you can begin to develop a personal playbook for navigating transitions, making each future change less daunting and more of an opportunity for growth.

Embracing the Learning Curve

Stepping into a new role or transitioning into a different industry often feels like entering a foreign landscape, where the rules, language, and expectations can be unfamiliar. This adjustment period, commonly referred to as the learning curve, is a natural and inevitable part of career growth. Despite its universal presence, the learning curve often triggers discomfort, frustration, and even insecurity. This section introduces the concept of the learning curve and why it plays such a central role in professional transitions. We will explore how approaching this phase with the right mindset can transform it from a period of struggle into an opportunity for accelerated development.

When faced with the unfamiliar, our minds are wired to perceive potential threats; this instinctual reaction stems from our evolutionary need to quickly adapt to new environments. In a workplace context, these perceived threats can take the form of unknown procedures, new team dynamics, or a different industry jargon. These challenges can amplify feelings of insecurity, leading many professionals to experience the "imposter syndrome," where they fear being exposed as less competent than their colleagues or superiors. However, it's essential to understand that the learning curve is not a reflection of our inadequacy but rather a natural phase of skill acquisition and adaptation. Instead of fearing it, embracing this curve as a normal, even expected, part of career transitions can help mitigate anxiety and foster a more productive mindset.

The steepness of the learning curve varies depending on factors such as the complexity of the new role, the level of change involved, and the individual's background. For instance, a seasoned professional switching industries might face a more challenging curve compared to someone moving into a familiar role within the same field. The good news is that this steep phase typically does not last forever. By understanding that the initial discomfort is temporary, professionals can better cope with the early challenges of the transition. Acknowledging that everyone experiences a learning curve can help reduce the pressure to perform flawlessly from day one. Recognizing this period as a chance to grow and expand one's capabilities reframes the discomfort as a valuable part of the learning process.

Moreover, viewing the learning curve through the lens of a growth mindset can make a significant difference in how individuals navigate transitions. A growth mindset, a concept popularized by psychologist Carol Dweck, posits that our abilities can be developed through effort, learning, and persistence. Rather than seeing gaps in knowledge as failures, those with a growth mindset perceive them as opportunities for development. By adopting this perspective, individuals can reframe the challenges they face as temporary hurdles rather than permanent roadblocks. This shift in outlook not only reduces the fear of making mistakes but also encourages a more proactive approach to seeking out new information, asking questions, and engaging in hands-on learning experiences.

The introduction to the learning curve is about setting expectations and normalizing the process of adaptation. It's a stage where humility becomes a valuable asset, allowing us to acknowledge what we don't know while remaining open to new experiences and knowledge. At the same time, it's crucial to pair humility with a sense of self-assurance, remembering that the skills and insights we've accumulated in past roles are still valuable and applicable, even if the context has changed. The challenge is not just to survive the learning curve but to embrace it as a catalyst for growth, setting the stage for long-term success in any new role or industry. This mindset shift—seeing the learning curve as an integral part of career advancement rather than an obstacle—is key to thriving through transitions.

Understanding the Need for Humility

In the fast-paced world of career transitions, humility might seem counterintuitive. Many believe that stepping into a new role or industry demands a show of confidence, competence, and an eagerness to prove oneself immediately. However, humility is a critical yet often overlooked trait that can significantly impact one's ability to adapt, learn, and ultimately thrive in a new environment. Understanding the need for humility during transitions is not about diminishing self-worth or playing small; instead, it's about recognizing the vast scope of what remains unknown and being open to new information, experiences, and perspectives. It is an active acknowledgment that there is always more to learn, no matter how experienced or skilled one might be.

Humility in this context is fundamentally about adopting a learner's mindset, one that prioritizes growth over immediate validation. When entering a new professional setting, the temptation to rely heavily on previous successes or established expertise can be strong. While past accomplishments provide a foundation of skills and confidence, they can also create blind spots if we are not careful. Clinging too tightly to what we already know may inhibit our capacity to absorb new insights or adapt to different approaches. In contrast, a humble approach facilitates curiosity and openness, fostering a willingness to question assumptions, ask clarifying questions, and seek guidance from others. It's about embracing the role of a student, even if you've already been a master in a previous context.

Humility also plays a vital role in building relationships during transitions. Entering a new team or industry often means working alongside people with different backgrounds, expertise, and perspectives. Displaying humility helps break down barriers and encourages a more collaborative atmosphere. Colleagues are more likely to respond positively to someone who shows a genuine interest in learning from them rather than someone who assumes they have all the answers. This openness can lead to stronger connections, more effective teamwork, and a richer exchange of ideas. It signals respect for the expertise of others, creating an environment where everyone feels valued and recognized. By demonstrating humility, you are effectively inviting others into your learning process, which can deepen trust and foster a shared commitment to mutual success.

Importantly, humility does not equate to a lack of confidence. This is a common misconception that can lead professionals to resist adopting a humble approach, fearing it might be perceived as a sign of weakness or incompetence. However, true humility is rooted in self-assurance. It involves knowing your strengths and recognizing your achievements while being aware of the limits of your current knowledge in a new context. It's the confidence to admit when you don't have the answers and the willingness to seek help or feedback. This blend of humility and confidence is powerful, as it allows you to navigate the learning curve without succumbing to the pressures of unrealistic self-expectations. It reflects a deeper self-awareness and a realistic understanding of the dynamic nature of career growth.

In many ways, humility is the bridge between self-assurance and adaptability. It tempers the ego, making room for new ideas and experiences that can enhance our skill set. Instead of approaching the new role with a fixed mindset that prioritizes proving our worth, humility encourages us to adopt a flexible, exploratory mindset. This shift in approach can make the transition process smoother, as it reduces the pressure to perform perfectly and allows for more authentic engagement with the learning process. By understanding the need for humility, professionals can approach transitions with a balanced perspective— one that honors past expertise while making space for new growth. In essence, it is about embracing the unknown with both courage and grace, understanding that true mastery comes from a willingness to remain a student throughout one's career.

CULTIVATING CONFIDENT HUMILITY

Cultivating confident humility is the art of balancing self-assurance with an openness to growth—a duality that is essential for navigating career transitions successfully. This nuanced approach requires individuals to embrace both the strength of their expertise and the vulnerability of acknowledging what they have yet to learn. Unlike false modesty, which masks insecurity with a veneer of humility, or overconfidence, which can alienate colleagues and stifle personal growth, confident humility represents a grounded sense of self. It is rooted in a realistic appraisal of one's capabilities and limitations, enabling professionals to navigate new environments with clarity and adaptability.

Confident humility starts with a strong sense of self-awareness. This means having a clear understanding of your core strengths, experiences, and unique skill set while also recognizing the areas where you might lack familiarity or need further development. For instance, when stepping into a new role or industry, the tasks and expectations may differ from those previously encountered. Here, confident humility allows you to assert your knowledge where it applies while remaining receptive to new methodologies or strategies specific to your new context. It's about using your past experiences as a sturdy foundation, not as a rigid script. This mindset fosters a dynamic approach to problem-solving, where you can confidently contribute insights without being constrained by the fear of not knowing everything.

One of the key practices in cultivating confident humility is the intentional effort to remain curious and ask questions without feeling diminished by the process. In many professional settings, there is an unspoken pressure to appear competent at all times, which can discourage inquiry and foster a culture of silent struggle. Confident humility challenges this norm by reframing questions not as signs of weakness but as tools for deeper understanding and growth. Leaders who exemplify this approach often set the tone for their teams by openly admitting when they don't have all the answers and actively seeking input from others. This behavior not only enhances their own learning but also creates a psychologically safe environment where team members feel empowered to share their knowledge and perspectives. By normalizing the act of seeking help or clarification, confident humility shifts the focus from individual ego to collective progress.

Another essential aspect of cultivating confident humility is the ability to receive feedback constructively. When we are overly concerned with projecting an image of infallibility, we can become defensive or dismissive in the face of criticism. However, a mindset rooted in confident humility views feedback as a valuable resource rather than a personal attack. It's an opportunity to gain insights into areas for improvement that might not be immediately visible to us. Embracing feedback in this way requires a deep sense of security in one's worth, recognizing that constructive criticism does not negate our accomplishments but rather complements them by pointing out new directions for growth. Practicing gratitude for feedback, even when it is challenging, is a sign of confident humility. It demonstrates the willingness to evolve and refine one's approach continually.

Cultivating confident humility also involves a commitment to lifelong learning. Professionals who embrace this quality view their careers as a journey of ongoing discovery rather than a destination of fixed achievements. This mindset encourages them to stay engaged, seek out new knowledge, and continuously hone their skills, even after reaching senior levels of expertise. They understand that every transition, whether it's a new job, a shift in responsibilities, or a move into a different industry, is an invitation to expand their capabilities and adapt to changing landscapes. By maintaining an attitude of confident humility, they avoid the stagnation that can come from complacency or rigidly clinging to past successes. Instead, they remain agile, ready to pivot and learn as new challenges arise, positioning themselves as adaptable and resilient leaders in any environment.

Confident humility is about harmonizing two seemingly opposing forces: the assurance that comes from knowing your value and the openness to admit when you need to learn more. It's a skill that can be cultivated through self-reflection, a willingness to engage in continuous learning, and the courage to show vulnerability in professional settings. When mastered, confident humility allows individuals to navigate transitions not with a false sense of bravado, but with a steady, grounded confidence that inspires trust and respect from others. This approach not only facilitates smoother career shifts but also enhances personal fulfillment, as it aligns with an authentic, growth-oriented way of being. It's a powerful tool for any professional looking to thrive in an ever-evolving career landscape.

PRACTICAL STRATEGIES FOR EMBRACING THE LEARNING CURVE

To effectively embrace the learning curve during a career transition, it is crucial to develop a set of practical strategies that empower you to approach new challenges with confidence and adaptability. These strategies involve a combination of mindset shifts, active learning methods, and the cultivation of key professional habits that make the process of acquiring new skills and knowledge more manageable and rewarding. By integrating these approaches, you can minimize the stress often associated with the steep learning curves of new roles while maximizing your potential for growth and success.

One foundational strategy for embracing the learning curve is to actively prioritize learning over performance in the initial phase of any transition. This mindset shift acknowledges that the early stages of a new job or industry are more about adaptation than immediate mastery. Instead of feeling pressured to prove yourself right away, focus on understanding the landscape: observe team dynamics, absorb the company culture, and familiarize yourself with key processes and tools. This approach requires patience and a willingness to be a beginner again, even if you have extensive experience in other areas. By lowering the self-imposed expectation of immediate expertise, you free yourself to ask questions and explore without the fear of appearing incompetent. This phase of active observation and inquiry sets a strong foundation for deeper learning and informed decision-making down the line.

Another effective tactic is to employ a deliberate learning plan tailored to the specific demands of your new role. This plan should include setting clear, incremental goals that break down the broader learning curve into manageable milestones. For example, if you are transitioning into a new industry, your first goal might be to familiarize yourself with the key terminology and industry-specific jargon. Following that, you might focus on understanding the major players, market trends, and the unique challenges facing your new sector. By setting these smaller, specific objectives, you create a roadmap that provides structure to your learning process and allows you to track your progress. This strategy also helps to alleviate the overwhelming feeling that can come from trying to absorb too much information at once. Celebrating these small wins along the way reinforces your confidence and builds momentum as you continue to climb the learning curve.

Engaging in active learning techniques is another practical approach to mastering the learning curve. Passive methods, such as reading or listening to presentations, can be helpful but are often less effective than strategies that require active participation. One of the most powerful active learning techniques is to teach what you've learned to others. When you attempt to explain a concept or process to a colleague, you are forced to organize your thoughts and clarify your understanding. Teaching can reveal gaps in your knowledge, prompting you to seek out additional information and refine your comprehension. This method, often referred to as the "Feynman technique," accelerates learning by encouraging you to think critically about the material. Additionally, engaging in role-playing scenarios or simulations relevant to your new role can provide a safe environment to practice skills and test your knowledge without the pressure of real-world consequences.

Seeking feedback early and often is another key strategy for embracing the learning curve effectively. Constructive feedback from colleagues, managers, or mentors can provide valuable insights that help you adjust your approach and avoid potential pitfalls. Instead of waiting for formal performance reviews, actively request informal check-ins or mentoring sessions where you can discuss your progress and ask for specific guidance. This proactive approach not only helps you learn faster but also demonstrates a growth mindset to your peers and supervisors. When seeking feedback, focus on specific areas where you feel less confident or are encountering difficulties, rather than asking broad, general questions. This targeted request for feedback shows that you are serious about your development and willing to take actionable steps to improve. It also helps you build stronger relationships with your colleagues, as it signals your respect for their expertise and your openness to learning.

Lastly, building a habit of consistent reflection is crucial for sustaining your progress along the learning curve. Reflection involves regularly taking time to assess what you have learned, what challenges you faced, and how you can adjust your strategies moving forward. One effective method is to maintain a learning journal where you document key insights, experiences, and lessons. This practice not only helps consolidate your knowledge but also serves as a tangible record of your growth. Reviewing your journal periodically allows you to see the progress you've made, which can be a powerful motivator when the learning curve feels particularly steep. Additionally, reflection helps you identify patterns in your learning process, such as common obstacles or recurring themes, enabling you to fine-tune your strategies and approach future challenges with greater ease.

Incorporating these practical strategies into your transition process equips you with the tools needed to embrace the learning curve with both humility and confidence. By prioritizing learning, creating a deliberate plan, engaging in active learning, seeking targeted feedback, and practicing reflection, you transform the challenge of a steep learning curve into an opportunity for substantial personal and professional growth. These habits not only enhance your adaptability in the short term but also lay the groundwork for continuous improvement throughout your career.

THE ROLE OF FEEDBACK AND ITERATIVE GROWTH

In the context of navigating a steep learning curve during career transitions, feedback plays a critical role as both a guide and a catalyst for growth. At its core, feedback provides an external perspective that helps refine our self-assessment, offering insights into areas where our perception of competence might not align with reality. This external input is invaluable, especially when stepping into new roles or industries where the standards, expectations, and skills required differ from previous experiences. Embracing feedback, however, is not merely about passively receiving critique; it involves actively seeking out constructive insights, processing them effectively, and using them as a springboard for iterative growth.

The importance of feedback during transitions cannot be overstated. When entering unfamiliar professional territory, it's common to face uncertainty and self-doubt. Without external validation or correction, it's easy to fall into the trap of either underestimating your progress or, conversely, overlooking critical gaps in your knowledge. Seeking feedback early helps to mitigate this risk by providing a more accurate gauge of your current abilities. In new roles, the feedback loop can be particularly valuable in helping you adjust your approach, clarify any misconceptions, and align more closely with the expectations of your team or organization. Feedback acts as a navigational tool, offering course corrections that keep you on track as you climb the learning curve, preventing you from straying too far off course in your efforts to adapt.

To fully leverage the benefits of feedback, it is essential to approach it with a growth mindset. A growth mindset, as defined by psychologist Carol Dweck, is the belief that abilities and intelligence can be developed through dedication and hard work. This perspective is especially relevant when adapting to new roles, as it encourages you to view feedback not as a judgment of your inherent abilities, but as an opportunity for learning and improvement. Embracing a growth mindset transforms feedback from something to be feared into a valuable resource that propels your progress. When you receive criticism or suggestions, instead of defensively justifying your actions or feeling disheartened, a growth mindset helps you to remain open and curious. You begin to see the feedback as a puzzle to solve: What can I learn from this? How can I apply these insights to enhance my performance? This approach fosters a sense of resilience and adaptability, which are crucial when tackling the challenges of a new job or industry.

A key component of effectively utilizing feedback is the concept of iterative growth. Iterative growth refers to the process of making small, continuous adjustments based on the feedback you receive, rather than expecting immediate, sweeping improvements. This method is akin to the agile approach often used in software development, where projects are completed in incremental stages, with regular evaluations and refinements along the way. By applying this concept to personal and professional development, you allow yourself the space to make gradual, sustainable progress. For instance, instead of attempting to master all aspects of your new role at once, focus on a single area of improvement highlighted in the feedback. Work on refining this skill or behavior over a set period, then reassess your progress before moving on to the next focus area. This iterative approach not only makes the learning process more manageable but also builds a sense of accomplishment as you see tangible results from each cycle of improvement.

Cultivating a habit of requesting specific, targeted feedback is another practical way to enhance your growth during transitions. Vague or generic feedback, such as "You're doing great" or "You need to improve," is of limited use when you are trying to climb a steep learning curve. Instead, aim to ask for detailed input on particular aspects of your performance. For example, if you've just presented a new idea to your team, rather than simply asking, "How did I do?" you could ask, "Was my explanation clear, or did you feel there were any points that needed further clarification?" or "How could I have structured my argument more effectively?" This type of request not only yields more actionable insights but also signals to your colleagues and managers that you are genuinely committed to improving and open to constructive criticism. Over time, this practice of seeking targeted feedback becomes a powerful tool for continuous learning and professional development.

The effective use of feedback during transitions requires a balance between internal reflection and external input. While feedback provides valuable external guidance, it's equally important to take time for self-reflection, analyzing how the feedback fits within your broader personal and career goals. This process of integrating feedback involves sifting through the input to identify what resonates and aligns with your vision of growth, and what might be less relevant or context-specific. Not every piece of feedback will be equally useful, and part of developing confident humility is learning to discern which critiques to act upon and which to take with a grain of salt. By blending external feedback with internal reflection, you create a comprehensive approach to learning that is both dynamic and grounded in self-awareness. This iterative cycle of feedback, reflection, and adjustment is what ultimately transforms the daunting experience of a steep learning curve into a rewarding journey of personal and professional growth.

INTEGRATING FEEDBACK FOR SUSTAINED GROWTH

Effectively integrating feedback is one of the most critical aspects of thriving through the challenges of a steep learning curve. It's easy to view feedback as a one-way street—something passively received and judged—but to leverage its full potential, it must be seen as an active, iterative process. Feedback serves as a mirror, reflecting areas of strength and highlighting blind spots you might otherwise overlook, especially when entering a new role or industry. During transitions, the ability to interpret and act upon feedback quickly can set the pace for your adaptation, helping you to avoid prolonged periods of uncertainty and boosting your confidence in tackling new tasks. The feedback loop becomes a dynamic process of trial, error, and refinement, where each cycle informs your next steps, enabling you to build momentum and competence as you settle into unfamiliar environments.

One of the most effective ways to integrate feedback is by approaching it with a mindset oriented toward iterative growth. Instead of expecting perfection immediately or becoming overwhelmed by the sheer volume of adjustments needed, breaking down the feedback into smaller, manageable actions can make the process less daunting. This method mirrors the principles of agile development, where improvements are made in incremental steps rather than attempting an overhaul all at once. Applying this to your professional growth means focusing on one or two specific areas highlighted in the feedback and setting measurable goals for improvement in those areas. For instance, if a manager notes that your presentations lack clarity, you might decide to focus on structuring your arguments more concisely in your next few meetings. By taking small, focused steps, you can build a sense of progress, which reinforces your confidence and helps sustain motivation throughout the transition period.

A proactive approach to seeking feedback can further enhance your growth during transitions. Many individuals fall into the trap of waiting for formal performance reviews or unsolicited comments from managers and colleagues, but by then, the opportunity for real-time improvement may have passed. Instead, consider actively soliciting feedback at key points during projects or tasks, particularly when experimenting with new methods or stepping into unfamiliar responsibilities. Being specific in your requests for feedback can yield more useful and targeted insights. For example, instead of a general inquiry like, "How am I doing?" try asking, "Did my report meet your expectations, or are there specific areas where I can improve my analysis?" This level of specificity not only encourages more actionable responses but also signals to your peers and superiors that you are invested in your development. Over time, this proactive habit fosters a culture of openness and continuous learning, which can significantly accelerate your adjustment to new roles.

The process of integrating feedback also requires a balance of external input and self-reflection. While it is essential to consider the perspectives of managers, colleagues, and mentors, not all feedback will align with your personal values or the direction you wish to take in your career. Developing the discernment to evaluate feedback critically allows you to decide which pieces of advice to act on and which to set aside. Self-reflection plays a key role here, providing the necessary space to process the feedback, assess its relevance, and integrate it into your broader professional goals. Taking time to reflect on the feedback you receive—whether through journaling, discussing it with a trusted mentor, or simply taking a moment to pause and think—can help you identify patterns and recurring themes. These insights not only guide your next steps but also help you understand how your efforts are perceived, giving you a clearer roadmap for ongoing improvement.

Incorporating feedback effectively during transitions is not just about making immediate changes; it's about establishing a habit of continual learning that extends beyond the initial adjustment phase. This ongoing practice of seeking, reflecting on, and acting upon feedback becomes a core component of your professional development strategy. It allows you to stay agile, adapting your approach as new challenges arise, and ultimately shortens the time it takes to find your footing in a new environment. By viewing feedback as a tool for growth rather than a measure of deficiency, you transform it into a powerful ally in your career journey, enabling you to build confidence and capability even in the face of steep learning curves.

Chapter 4: Promoting Yourself Without Fear

Self-advocacy is a pivotal yet often misunderstood aspect of career growth. Many professionals shy away from promoting their achievements, fearing they might come across as boastful or self-centered. However, advocating for oneself is not about arrogance—it's about ensuring that your contributions are recognized and valued. Without this skill, even the most competent individuals risk being overlooked for promotions, raises, or leadership opportunities.

Consider the story of Maria, a diligent and skilled project manager. Despite her exceptional performance, she watched a colleague with less experience get promoted over her. When Maria sought feedback, her supervisor mentioned that her contributions, while impressive, weren't as visible as others'. This revelation hit her hard. Maria had assumed her hard work would speak for itself, but in reality, she had missed opportunities to highlight her accomplishments and their impact on the organization.

This chapter aims to shift your perspective on self-advocacy. Far from being self-serving, it is a professional responsibility that benefits both you and your organization. By effectively communicating your value, you not only position yourself for advancement but also help your team and leadership make informed decisions about allocating talent and resources.

Cultural and societal influences may have taught you to "wait for recognition" or to believe that good work will inevitably be noticed. While commendable in theory, this mindset often backfires in competitive workplaces. The reality is that visibility matters, and self-advocacy is the bridge between your hard work and the recognition you deserve.

Through this chapter, you'll learn practical strategies to confidently discuss your achievements, ask for promotions, and navigate conversations about career growth without fear of judgment or rejection. Whether you're a seasoned professional or just starting out, mastering self-advocacy will empower you to take charge of your career trajectory. Let's begin by understanding how to present your value effectively.

PRACTICAL TIPS FOR DISCUSSING ACHIEVEMENTS AND ASKING FOR PROMOTIONS

Discussing your achievements and asking for promotions is an art that balances confidence, preparation, and strategic communication. It requires you to not only recognize your contributions but also articulate them in a way that aligns with organizational goals. While many professionals assume that their work will naturally speak for itself, the truth is that visibility often requires deliberate effort. Your accomplishments may be remarkable, but if they remain unnoticed, their value diminishes in the eyes of decision-makers. Learning to present your successes effectively is the first step toward career advancement.

The key to discussing your achievements lies in framing them as contributions to the larger success of your team or organization. This approach shifts the focus away from self-promotion and positions your work as a shared victory. For instance, instead of saying, "I completed a major project ahead of schedule," try, "The project I led saved the company three weeks in production time, allowing us to launch before our competitors." This not only highlights your role but also connects it to measurable outcomes that benefit the company. A useful framework for crafting such narratives is the "Challenge-Action-Result" model, where you briefly outline the problem, the steps you took to address it, and the results you achieved.

Timing and context are equally important when asking for promotions. While performance reviews and one-on-one meetings are common opportunities, they aren't the only moments to advocate for yourself. Pay attention to milestones in your work—such as the successful completion of a major project or a significant contribution to a team goal—as natural openings for these conversations. Before initiating the discussion, prepare thoroughly by aligning your achievements with the company's priorities. Show how your growth aligns with the organization's objectives, and frame your promotion as a logical step that benefits not only you but also your team and leadership.

Practicing these conversations is essential. The fear of stumbling or saying the wrong thing often holds people back, but preparation can help you overcome this hesitation. Rehearse your key points with a trusted friend, mentor, or coach who can provide constructive feedback. Pay attention to your tone and language—be assertive yet respectful. For example, rather than saying, "I think I've done a good job," say, "I'm proud of my work on [specific project], which resulted in [specific outcome]. I'd like to discuss how I can continue contributing at a higher level." Practicing this balance of confidence and humility ensures that you approach these discussions with clarity and poise. When done right, discussing achievements and asking for promotions can be transformative, unlocking new opportunities and enhancing your professional credibility.

OVERCOMING FEAR OF JUDGMENT WHEN SPEAKING UP

Fear of judgment is one of the most common barriers to self-advocacy. Many professionals hesitate to speak up, worried about how their words might be perceived or whether they might inadvertently invite criticism. This fear often stems from a mix of personal insecurities, past experiences, and societal conditioning. For example, some people were raised in environments where humility was overemphasized, leading them to believe that drawing attention to their own achievements is inappropriate. Others might have experienced negative feedback in the past, reinforcing a reluctance to assert themselves. While these fears are valid, they can significantly limit career growth if left unaddressed.

To overcome the fear of judgment, it's important to reframe self-advocacy as sharing information rather than boasting. When you speak up about your achievements or ideas, you're providing valuable insights that others might not have considered. Viewing self-advocacy as a contribution to the team or organization shifts the focus away from self-centeredness and toward collective benefit. For instance, when proposing an idea in a meeting, you might preface it with, "I'd like to share a perspective that could help us approach this challenge more effectively," emphasizing the value of your input rather than drawing attention to yourself.

Building confidence in speaking up also requires incremental exposure. Start small by advocating for yourself in low-stakes situations, such as suggesting a minor improvement in a routine process or volunteering to lead a small project. These smaller acts of self-advocacy serve as stepping stones, helping you build the confidence needed for more significant discussions. Each successful attempt reinforces your ability to advocate effectively, making the prospect of judgment feel less intimidating. Over time, this gradual approach can transform how you perceive and handle such interactions.

Another strategy is to reframe potential feedback as an opportunity for growth rather than a personal attack. It's natural to fear criticism, but constructive feedback can help refine your ideas and enhance your professional development. When you speak up and receive feedback, consider it a sign that your input was valuable enough to merit discussion. Instead of interpreting judgment as a negative outcome, view it as an essential part of collaboration and learning. By embracing feedback and focusing on the value of your contributions, you can diminish the fear of judgment and build a habit of self-advocacy that supports your long-term career growth.

TOOLS AND RESOURCES

Effective self-advocacy requires preparation, practice, and access to the right tools. These tools not only help you organize your thoughts and achievements but also give you a structured approach to navigating potentially intimidating conversations. When you equip yourself with the proper resources, you can transform moments of hesitation into opportunities for growth and recognition. This section provides actionable frameworks, checklists, and exercises that you can immediately apply to strengthen your self-advocacy skills.

One essential resource is a **self-advocacy checklist** designed to guide you through key steps before discussing achievements or requesting a promotion. Start by documenting your contributions with a focus on measurable outcomes. This might involve writing down recent accomplishments, the specific challenges you addressed, and the results of your actions. For example, instead of stating, "I worked on the marketing campaign," highlight, "I led the marketing campaign that increased engagement by 30% within three months." Connecting your achievements to quantifiable results demonstrates your value clearly and effectively.

Once you've documented your accomplishments, align them with the organization's goals. Consider what your team or company is striving to achieve and identify how your contributions have supported these objectives. Framing your work within this broader context helps decision-makers see you as someone who drives success on a larger scale. For instance, if your company is focused on improving efficiency, highlight how you streamlined a process or saved time and resources. Use this alignment to build a compelling narrative that makes your request for advancement feel logical and well-timed.

Practicing your delivery is another critical tool for effective self-advocacy. Role-playing scenarios with a trusted colleague, friend, or mentor can help you refine your language, tone, and confidence. During these practice sessions, focus on maintaining assertiveness while staying respectful and collaborative. For example, rehearse saying, "I'm proud of the results I achieved on [specific project] and believe my skills align with the responsibilities of [desired role]. I'd like to explore opportunities to contribute at that level." By rehearsing key phrases and scenarios, you can minimize anxiety and approach real conversations with greater clarity and poise.

Lastly, templates and scripts are invaluable resources for structuring your discussions. Whether you're preparing for a one-on-one meeting with your manager or planning to speak up in a team setting, having a clear outline of what to say can make the process less daunting. For example, a promotion request script might include:

1. A brief introduction outlining your intent (e.g., "I'd like to discuss how I can continue contributing to the team's success in a more advanced role.")

2. A summary of your achievements using the Challenge-Action-Result framework.

3. A forward-looking statement that ties your growth to organizational goals (e.g., "I'm excited about the opportunity to take on new responsibilities that align with our strategic priorities.")

By using these tools and resources, you can develop a systematic approach to self-advocacy that feels natural and achievable. The more you practice and refine these methods, the more confident and effective you will become in advocating for yourself in any professional setting.

Let me share the story of Daniel, a software engineer who spent years excelling in his role without receiving the recognition he deserved. Daniel was known for his meticulous work and problem-solving skills, but he often struggled to speak up about his achievements. Like many professionals, he believed that hard work would naturally lead to advancement, and he feared that self-advocacy might come across as self-serving or arrogant.

One day, Daniel faced a turning point. His team had just completed a high-stakes project under his quiet yet decisive leadership, significantly reducing downtime for a critical system. While his manager praised the team's success during a meeting, Daniel's contributions weren't explicitly mentioned. Feeling frustrated but determined, Daniel decided it was time to advocate for himself. He prepared for a one-on-one meeting with his manager by documenting his role in the project, focusing on measurable outcomes such as the 20% reduction in system downtime and the cost savings it generated.

During the meeting, Daniel approached the conversation with a balance of confidence and humility. He began by expressing gratitude for being part of a supportive team and then outlined his specific contributions to the project. Using the Challenge-Action-Result framework, he described the technical hurdles he overcame, the innovative solutions he implemented, and their impact on the company's operations. He concluded by expressing his desire to take on more leadership responsibilities and exploring how he could grow within the organization.

Daniel's advocacy paid off. His manager not only recognized his contributions but also praised his initiative in seeking growth opportunities. Within weeks, Daniel was offered a promotion to lead a new team tackling high-priority projects. This recognition boosted his confidence and marked the beginning of a career where he no longer hesitated to share his value. Reflecting on the experience, Daniel realized that advocating for oneself isn't about self-promotion—it's about ensuring that the work you do receives the acknowledgment it deserves, benefiting both you and your organization.

Daniel's journey is a powerful reminder that overcoming the fear of self-advocacy can unlock transformative opportunities. His story shows that when you prepare thoughtfully, communicate clearly, and align your contributions with organizational goals, you can confidently advocate for yourself without fear of judgment. Most importantly, it reinforces the idea that self-advocacy isn't just a skill—it's a form of empowerment that allows you to shape your career trajectory and achieve the recognition you've earned.

Networking with Confidence

Networking is often regarded as a cornerstone of professional success, yet its significance is frequently misunderstood or undervalued. Primarily, networking is about building relationships—fostering connections with people who can offer insights, collaboration opportunities, or mentorship. More importantly, it's a two-way street; successful networking is as much about what you can offer others as it is about what they can offer you. In the modern workplace, where opportunities often arise from relationships rather than job boards, networking can make the difference between stagnation and career growth.

For many professionals, the term "networking" conjures up images of transactional, superficial interactions at crowded events or awkward LinkedIn messages. This perception leads to hesitation, as people fear appearing inauthentic or self-serving. However, true networking is not about collecting business cards or seeking favors; it's about forming genuine, mutually beneficial relationships. When approached with authenticity and curiosity, networking becomes a powerful tool for personal and professional development, creating lasting partnerships rather than fleeting acquaintances.

One of the most important roles networking plays in career success is providing access to opportunities that might otherwise remain hidden. Many job openings are filled through internal recommendations or informal channels before they're ever advertised. A strong professional network ensures that you're in the loop when these opportunities arise. Additionally, connections can offer valuable guidance, whether it's industry-specific advice, insights into company culture, or mentorship for navigating challenges. Through networking, you gain access to perspectives and knowledge that help you make more informed career decisions.

Beyond opening doors to new roles or projects, networking fosters growth by surrounding you with individuals who inspire and challenge you. When you connect with people who share your aspirations or possess expertise you admire, you create an environment where growth is inevitable. These relationships encourage you to think differently, learn continuously, and remain adaptable in a fast-evolving workplace. In this sense, networking is not merely a professional activity; it's an investment in your long-term personal and career development.

UNDERSTANDING NETWORKING ANXIETY

Networking anxiety is an obstacle many professionals face, often rooted in deeply ingrained fears and misconceptions. For some, the thought of initiating conversations with strangers or presenting themselves in a professional setting triggers self-doubt and insecurity. This discomfort can stem from a fear of judgment—worrying about being perceived as overly ambitious, awkward, or uninteresting. For others, the anxiety arises from overthinking every interaction, dissecting what to say, how to say it, and how the other person might respond. Understanding the origins and dynamics of this anxiety is the first step toward overcoming it.

One of the primary drivers of networking anxiety is a fear of rejection. Reaching out to someone for guidance, advice, or a professional connection makes you vulnerable, as the other person might decline, ignore, or dismiss your efforts. This fear is often magnified for individuals who struggle with imposter syndrome or insecurity, as they may feel they have little to offer in a networking exchange. The anticipation of rejection can become so paralyzing that many avoid networking altogether, missing out on valuable opportunities for growth and collaboration.

Another factor contributing to networking anxiety is the pressure to make a perfect impression. Professionals often place undue emphasis on crafting the ideal elevator pitch, maintaining flawless body language, or saying exactly the right thing to impress a potential connection. This perfectionism can lead to excessive rehearsing and second-guessing, creating a cycle of overthinking that prevents authentic interactions. Ironically, the more individuals focus on appearing polished, the harder it becomes to connect naturally with others, exacerbating feelings of inadequacy.

Social and cultural dynamics also play a role in networking anxiety. For individuals from underrepresented backgrounds or introverted personalities, traditional networking environments—such as loud events or hierarchical workplaces—may feel particularly alienating. These spaces often emphasize extroverted behaviors like small talk or self-promotion, which may not come naturally to everyone. Recognizing these systemic challenges is essential in reframing networking as an inclusive and adaptable practice. By understanding these anxieties and their underlying causes, professionals can begin to develop strategies to approach networking with greater confidence and ease.

PRACTICAL STRATEGIES FOR NETWORKING WITH CONFIDENCE

Networking with confidence begins with reframing your approach. Many professionals see networking as a daunting, high-stakes activity that requires flawless execution. This mindset often leads to anxiety, hesitation, or avoidance.

Instead, consider networking as an opportunity for mutual learning and connection. Shift the focus from proving your worth to discovering shared interests and exchanging ideas. This simple shift in perspective can significantly reduce the pressure and create a more relaxed, authentic dynamic during interactions.

Preparation is a key strategy for building confidence in networking situations. Researching the people, companies, or industries you're interested in before attending an event or initiating a conversation provides a sense of direction and readiness. Prepare a concise introduction or "elevator pitch" that highlights who you are and what you do in a natural, conversational tone. However, don't let over-preparation turn into rigidity. Instead, treat your preparation as a foundation that allows you to remain adaptable and engaged in the moment.

Active listening is another critical component of confident networking. Many people believe that networking requires dominating the conversation or dazzling others with their achievements. In reality, being an attentive listener is often more impactful than speaking at length about yourself. By asking thoughtful questions and genuinely engaging with what the other person is saying, you demonstrate curiosity and respect. This approach not only reduces the pressure on you but also fosters a sense of connection and reciprocity that lays the groundwork for a meaningful relationship.

Setting small, realistic goals for each networking interaction can help alleviate the overwhelm that often accompanies these situations. Rather than aiming to secure a job offer or a formal mentorship in a single conversation, focus on simpler objectives, such as learning about someone's career path, gaining insights into an industry trend, or exchanging contact information. Viewing networking as a series of manageable steps rather than a single monumental effort makes the process more approachable and helps build your confidence gradually over time.

BUILDING AUTHENTIC CONNECTIONS

Building authentic connections is the essence of effective networking. Authenticity is what transforms surface-level interactions into meaningful relationships that endure beyond a fleeting exchange. When you approach networking with the intention of fostering genuine connections rather than pursuing self-serving goals, you naturally create a foundation of trust and mutual respect. This authenticity makes you more approachable, memorable, and impactful in professional settings, as people are more likely to engage with someone who seems genuinely interested in them rather than focused solely on their own agenda.

The first step in building authentic connections is shifting your mindset from "What can I gain from this interaction?" to "How can I create value for this person?" This could mean sharing a helpful resource, offering encouragement, or simply listening attentively to their experiences. When you approach networking with generosity, the focus shifts away from your own anxieties, and the interaction feels more balanced. Authentic connections thrive when both parties feel seen, heard, and valued, so ensuring the other person's needs and interests are considered is key.

Another vital component of authenticity is vulnerability. While it's important to maintain professionalism, being open about your own challenges, aspirations, or learning experiences can make you more relatable. For instance, admitting that you're exploring a new career path or navigating a professional transition can encourage others to share their own experiences, creating a sense of camaraderie. Vulnerability fosters depth in conversations, moving them beyond surface-level topics like job titles or company names, and helps build rapport.

Consistency is what sustains authentic connections over time. Many people make the mistake of seeing networking as a one-time interaction rather than an ongoing relationship. Following up after an initial conversation, whether it's through a thank-you email, sharing a relevant article, or arranging a coffee chat, shows that you're invested in maintaining the connection. Authenticity in networking isn't about grand gestures or instant results; it's about cultivating trust and mutual support over time, turning brief encounters into valuable professional relationships.

OVERCOMING COMMON NETWORKING PITFALLS

Networking, despite its importance, often comes with potential missteps that can undermine efforts to build meaningful relationships. One of the most common pitfalls is treating networking as a transactional process. Approaching interactions solely with the aim of extracting benefits—be it job referrals, endorsements, or favors—can make conversations feel forced and one-sided. This approach often alienates others, as people sense when interactions lack genuine interest or reciprocity. Overcoming this pitfall requires a shift in mindset: focus on fostering mutual value rather than immediate gain, and prioritize building trust over time.

Another frequent challenge is over-reliance on scripted communication. While preparing for networking situations is valuable, sticking rigidly to a rehearsed pitch or list of questions can make interactions feel mechanical and impersonal. This often stems from a fear of saying the wrong thing, but paradoxically, it creates barriers to authentic connection. To avoid this, aim for adaptability in conversations. Be present and responsive to the other person's cues, allowing discussions to flow naturally rather than steering them toward predetermined outcomes.

Networking anxiety can also lead to over-apologizing or undervaluing your own contributions. For instance, some professionals might open conversations with statements like, "I'm sorry to bother you," or downplay their experience and skills to avoid seeming boastful. While humility is important, diminishing your worth can send the wrong message and undermine your confidence. Instead, approach networking with a balanced self-assurance, recognizing that you have value to offer. Replace apologies with gratitude—for example, thanking someone for their time or insights—which shifts the focus to appreciation rather than self-doubt.

Finally, a major pitfall is neglecting follow-up. Many professionals fail to maintain the momentum after an initial interaction, assuming the other person will take the next step or fearing they'll appear pushy. However, consistent follow-up is crucial to building long-term relationships. A thoughtful email, message, or coffee invitation can solidify the connection and demonstrate your sincerity. The key is to personalize your follow-ups, referencing specific topics from your conversation to show genuine engagement. Avoid generic or excessive communication, focusing instead on meaningful and periodic touchpoints. By addressing these common pitfalls, you can network with greater confidence, authenticity, and effectiveness.

DIGITAL NETWORKING IN A HYBRID WORLD

Networking is often regarded as a cornerstone of professional success, yet its significance is frequently misunderstood or undervalued. At its core, networking is about building relationships—fostering connections with people who can offer insights, collaboration opportunities, or mentorship. More importantly, it's a two-way street; successful networking is as much about what you can offer others as it is about what they can offer you. In the modern workplace, where opportunities often arise from relationships rather than job boards, networking can make the difference between stagnation and career growth.

For many professionals, the term "networking" conjures up images of transactional, superficial interactions at crowded events or awkward LinkedIn messages. This perception leads to hesitation, as people fear appearing inauthentic or self-serving. However, true networking is not about collecting business cards or seeking favors; it's about forming genuine, mutually beneficial relationships. When approached with authenticity and curiosity, networking becomes a powerful tool for personal and professional development, creating lasting partnerships rather than fleeting acquaintances.

One of the most important roles networking plays in career success is providing access to opportunities that might otherwise remain hidden. Many job openings are filled through internal recommendations or informal channels before they're ever advertised. A strong professional network ensures that you're in the loop when these opportunities arise. Additionally, connections can offer valuable guidance, whether it's industry-specific advice, insights into company culture, or mentorship for navigating challenges. Through networking, you gain access to perspectives and knowledge that help you make more informed career decisions.

Beyond opening doors to new roles or projects, networking fosters growth by surrounding you with individuals who inspire and challenge you. When you connect with people who share your aspirations or possess expertise you admire, you create an environment where growth is inevitable. These relationships encourage you to think differently, learn continuously, and remain adaptable in a fast-evolving workplace. In this sense, networking is not merely a professional activity; it's an investment in your long-term personal and career development.

UNDERSTANDING NETWORKING ANXIETY

Networking anxiety is an obstacle many professionals face, often rooted in deeply ingrained fears and misconceptions. For some, the thought of initiating conversations with strangers or presenting themselves in a professional setting triggers self-questioning and insecurity. This discomfort can stem from a fear of judgment—worrying about being perceived as overly ambitious, awkward, or uninteresting. For others, the anxiety arises from overthinking every interaction, dissecting what to say, how to say it, and how the other person might respond. Understanding the origins and dynamics of this anxiety is the first step toward overcoming it.

One of the primary drivers of networking anxiety is a fear of rejection. Reaching out to someone for guidance, advice, or a professional connection makes you vulnerable, as the other person might decline, ignore, or dismiss your efforts. This fear is often magnified for individuals who struggle with imposter syndrome or self-doubt, as they may feel they have little to offer in a networking exchange. The anticipation of rejection can become so paralyzing that many avoid networking altogether, missing out on valuable opportunities for growth and collaboration.

Another factor contributing to networking anxiety is the pressure to make a perfect impression. Professionals often place undue emphasis on crafting the ideal elevator pitch, maintaining flawless body language, or saying exactly the right thing to impress a potential connection. This perfectionism can lead to excessive rehearsing and second-guessing, creating a cycle of overthinking that prevents authentic interactions. Ironically, the more individuals focus on appearing polished, the harder it becomes to connect naturally with others, exacerbating feelings of inadequacy.

Social and cultural dynamics also play a role in networking anxiety. For individuals from underrepresented backgrounds or introverted personalities, traditional networking environments—such as loud events or hierarchical workplaces—may feel particularly alienating. These spaces often emphasize extroverted behaviors like small talk or self-promotion, which may not come naturally to everyone. Recognizing these systemic challenges is essential in reframing networking as an inclusive and adaptable practice. By understanding these anxieties and their underlying causes, professionals can begin to develop strategies to approach networking with greater confidence and ease.

PRACTICAL STRATEGIES FOR NETWORKING WITH CONFIDENCE

Networking with confidence begins with reframing your approach. Many professionals see networking as a daunting, high-stakes activity that requires flawless execution. This mindset often leads to anxiety, hesitation, or avoidance. Instead, consider networking as an opportunity for mutual learning and connection. Shift the focus from proving your worth to discovering shared interests and exchanging ideas. This simple shift in perspective can significantly reduce the pressure and create a more relaxed, authentic dynamic during interactions.

Preparation is a key strategy for building confidence in networking situations. Researching the people, companies, or industries you're interested in before attending an event or initiating a conversation provides a sense of direction and readiness. Prepare a concise introduction or "elevator pitch" that highlights who you are and what you do in a natural, conversational tone. However, don't let over-preparation turn into rigidity. Instead, treat your preparation as a foundation that allows you to remain adaptable and engaged in the moment.

Active listening is another critical component of confident networking. Many people believe that networking requires dominating the conversation or dazzling others with their achievements. In reality, being an attentive listener is often more impactful than speaking at length about yourself. By asking thoughtful questions and genuinely engaging with what the other person is saying, you demonstrate curiosity and respect. This approach not only reduces the pressure on you but also fosters a sense of connection and reciprocity that lays the groundwork for a meaningful relationship.

Setting small, realistic goals for each networking interaction can help alleviate the overwhelm that often accompanies these situations. Rather than aiming to secure a job offer or a formal mentorship in a single conversation, focus on simpler objectives, such as learning about someone's career path, gaining insights into an industry trend, or exchanging contact information. Viewing networking as a series of manageable steps rather than a single monumental effort makes the process more approachable and helps build your confidence gradually over time.

BUILDING AUTHENTIC CONNECTIONS

Building authentic connections is the essence of effective networking. Authenticity is what transforms surface-level interactions into meaningful relationships that endure beyond a fleeting exchange. When you approach networking with the intention of fostering genuine connections rather than pursuing self-serving goals, you naturally create a foundation of trust and mutual respect. This authenticity makes you more approachable, memorable, and impactful in professional settings, as people are more likely to engage with someone who seems genuinely interested in them rather than focused solely on their own agenda.

The first step in building authentic connections is shifting your mindset from "What can I gain from this interaction?" to "How can I create value for this person?" This could mean sharing a helpful resource, offering encouragement, or simply listening attentively to their experiences. When you approach networking with generosity, the focus shifts away from your own anxieties, and the interaction feels more balanced. Authentic connections thrive when both parties feel seen, heard, and valued, so ensuring the other person's needs and interests are considered is key.

Another vital component of authenticity is vulnerability. While it's important to maintain professionalism, being open about your own challenges, aspirations, or learning experiences can make you more relatable. For instance, admitting that you're exploring a new career path or navigating a professional transition can encourage others to share their own experiences, creating a sense of camaraderie. Vulnerability fosters depth in conversations, moving them beyond surface-level topics like job titles or company names, and helps build rapport.

Consistency is what sustains authentic connections over time. Many people make the mistake of seeing networking as a one-time interaction rather than an ongoing relationship. Following up after an initial conversation, whether it's through a thank-you email, sharing a relevant article, or arranging a coffee chat, shows that you're invested in maintaining the connection. Authenticity in networking isn't about grand gestures or instant results; it's about cultivating trust and mutual support over time, turning brief encounters into valuable professional relationships.

Overcoming Common Networking Pitfalls

Networking, despite its importance, often comes with potential missteps that can undermine efforts to build meaningful relationships. One of the most common pitfalls is treating networking as a transactional process. Approaching interactions solely with the aim of extracting benefits—be it job referrals, endorsements, or favors—can make conversations feel forced and one-sided. This approach often alienates others, as people sense when interactions lack genuine interest or reciprocity. Overcoming this pitfall requires a shift in mindset: focus on fostering mutual value rather than immediate gain, and prioritize building trust over time.

Another frequent challenge is over-reliance on scripted communication. While preparing for networking situations is valuable, sticking rigidly to a rehearsed pitch or list of questions can make interactions feel mechanical and impersonal. This often stems from a fear of saying the wrong thing, but paradoxically, it creates barriers to authentic connection. To avoid this, aim for adaptability in conversations. Be present and responsive to the other person's cues, allowing discussions to flow naturally rather than steering them toward predetermined outcomes.

Networking anxiety can also lead to over-apologizing or undervaluing your own contributions. For instance, some professionals might open conversations with statements like, "I'm sorry to bother you," or downplay their experience and skills to avoid seeming boastful. While humility is important, diminishing your worth can send the wrong message and undermine your confidence. Instead, approach networking with a balanced self-assurance, recognizing that you have value to offer. Replace apologies with gratitude—for example, thanking someone for their time or insights—which shifts the focus to appreciation rather than self-doubt.

Finally, a major pitfall is neglecting follow-up. Many professionals fail to maintain the momentum after an initial interaction, assuming the other person will take the next step or fearing they'll appear pushy. However, consistent follow-up is crucial to building long-term relationships. A thoughtful email, message, or coffee invitation can solidify the connection and demonstrate your sincerity. The key is to personalize your follow-ups, referencing specific topics from your conversation to show genuine engagement. Avoid generic or excessive communication, focusing instead on meaningful and periodic touchpoints. By addressing these common pitfalls, you can network with greater confidence, authenticity, and effectiveness.

DIGITAL NETWORKING IN A HYBRID WORLD

The rise of hybrid work environments has transformed networking, making digital interactions as vital as in-person connections. Virtual platforms like LinkedIn, professional forums, and industry-specific webinars have become the go-to spaces for professionals seeking to build relationships. While these tools offer convenience and accessibility, they also present unique challenges, such as establishing rapport without face-to-face interaction or navigating the nuances of online communication. Successfully networking in a hybrid world requires adapting to these changes while maintaining authenticity and intentionality.

One key strategy for effective digital networking is curating a strong and professional online presence. Your online profiles often serve as the first impression in the virtual world, making it essential to ensure they reflect your expertise and personality. A well-crafted LinkedIn profile, for example, should highlight your skills, achievements, and goals while also sharing a bit of your professional story. Engaging with others by posting thoughtful content, commenting on industry trends, or celebrating colleagues' achievements can further enhance your visibility and credibility, positioning you as a dynamic and approachable professional.

Initiating and maintaining online connections requires a slightly different approach than in-person interactions. In virtual settings, starting conversations often means sending a direct message or email, which can feel intimidating. To make this process smoother, tailor your outreach with a clear purpose. Reference a mutual connection, shared interest, or something specific about the person's work that caught your attention. For example, instead of sending a generic message, you might say, "I enjoyed your recent article on industry trends and found it insightful—would you be open to discussing this further over a quick call?" Thoughtful, personalized outreach fosters a sense of sincerity and increases the likelihood of a meaningful response.

Participating in virtual events is another powerful way to network in a hybrid world. These events—whether webinars, conferences, or online workshops— offer opportunities to interact with industry leaders and peers in a structured setting. During these events, engage actively by asking questions, participating in chat discussions, or following up with speakers and attendees afterward. The hybrid model also enables creative combinations of virtual and in-person networking; for instance, you might connect online with someone you plan to meet at an upcoming conference, creating a foundation for a more impactful face-to-face interaction.

Successful digital networking relies on consistency and follow-through. Unlike in-person encounters, digital connections often require more effort to nurture and sustain. Regularly check in with your network by sharing relevant articles, congratulating them on achievements, or simply expressing interest in their work. By staying active and engaged online, you can build lasting relationships that transcend the digital realm, ensuring your professional network remains robust and supportive in an increasingly hybrid workplace.

INSPIRATIONAL CASE STUDY: NETWORKING AS A CATALYST FOR GROWTH

Consider the story of Priya, a mid-career professional in the tech industry, who used networking to completely transform her career. Priya had spent nearly a decade as a software developer, excelling in technical skills but feeling stuck in her role. Despite her achievements, she hesitated to seek leadership opportunities, believing she lacked the charisma and connections required for management. Networking seemed intimidating, and Priya worried that she had nothing valuable to offer in professional conversations.

A turning point came when Priya attended a virtual industry panel during the pandemic. Inspired by one of the speakers—a female CTO who shared her journey of breaking barriers in tech—Priya decided to reach out. Though nervous, she sent a thoughtful LinkedIn message expressing her admiration and curiosity about the speaker's path. To her surprise, the CTO responded warmly, inviting her to a follow-up chat. That initial conversation provided not only inspiration but also practical advice on how to transition into leadership roles and make her presence known in the industry.

Encouraged by this interaction, Priya began to approach networking differently. She joined online communities for women in tech, actively participated in discussions, and even volunteered to co-host a virtual panel. These efforts helped her expand her network and build confidence in her ability to contribute. One connection led to another, and soon Priya found herself in touch with a senior executive at a startup looking for engineering leaders. They appreciated her technical expertise and proactive engagement in the tech community, offering her a leadership role that aligned with her aspirations.

Today, Priya is not only thriving in her new position but has also become a vocal advocate for empowering others through networking. She often shares her story at events, emphasizing the value of stepping out of one's comfort zone to build authentic relationships. Priya's journey underscores a powerful lesson: networking is not about being the most extroverted or accomplished person in the room—it's about showing genuine curiosity, embracing opportunities to connect, and recognizing the mutual value that relationships bring. Her experience demonstrates how a single act of reaching out can set off a chain reaction of growth and opportunity, proving that networking truly is a catalyst for career transformation.

ACTIONABLE TAKEAWAYS AND EXERCISES

Building a robust network requires both practical strategies and deliberate effort. The following actionable takeaways and exercises are designed to help you apply the principles of confident and authentic networking to your professional journey. By practicing these steps consistently, you can transform networking from a daunting task into a natural and rewarding habit.

Set Intentional Networking Goals

Start by defining your networking objectives. Are you looking to explore a new industry, find a mentor, or gain insight into specific roles? Write down two or three clear goals that align with your career aspirations. For each goal, identify potential people, events, or platforms that can help you achieve it. For example, if you aim to transition into marketing, consider attending industry webinars or reaching out to professionals on LinkedIn who specialize in that field. This exercise provides focus and prevents aimless networking.

Create and Practice Your Introduction

Develop a concise and authentic personal introduction that highlights your professional identity and aspirations. Use the following structure:

1. Who you are: "I'm a project manager specializing in technology-driven solutions."

2. What you do: "I focus on streamlining workflows and improving team collaboration."

3. Why you're connecting: "I'm exploring strategies for transitioning to leadership roles and would love to hear about your journey."

Practice delivering this introduction naturally with friends or colleagues until it feels conversational. Revisiting and refining your introduction periodically will ensure it evolves with your career.

Start Small with Outreach

Networking doesn't require grand gestures. Begin with manageable steps, such as reconnecting with former colleagues or commenting thoughtfully on someone's LinkedIn post. For example, send a brief message to a past coworker saying, "I recently saw your update about your new role—congratulations! I'd love to hear about your transition sometime." Consistently engaging with your network builds confidence and strengthens relationships over time.

Role-Playing Conversations

If networking anxiety holds you back, try role-playing scenarios with a trusted friend or mentor. Practice initiating conversations, asking questions, and responding to common scenarios, such as discussing shared interests or handling rejection. For instance, simulate an event where you need to introduce yourself to a stranger, and take turns offering constructive feedback. This exercise helps desensitize you to the stress of networking situations and equips you with practical dialogue tools.

Track and Reflect on Progress

Keep a networking journal to document your interactions, insights, and areas for improvement. After each event or conversation, jot down what went well and what could be enhanced. For example, did you engage actively? Were you able to follow up effectively? Over time, this practice will reveal patterns, highlight your growth, and help you refine your approach.

By implementing these exercises and maintaining consistent effort, you'll not only develop stronger networking skills but also build the confidence and connections necessary to thrive in your professional journey. Networking is a skill that grows with practice, and each step forward strengthens your ability to connect meaningfully with others.

Chapter 5: Overcoming the Comparison Trap

Social media platforms have become an integral part of our professional lives, especially tools like LinkedIn that promise to connect us with opportunities, expand our networks, and showcase our achievements. For many professionals, logging onto these platforms is a routine task, a means of staying visible in an increasingly competitive world. Yet, beneath the surface of polished profiles and congratulatory posts lies a profound and often unspoken challenge: the impact of curated success stories on self-esteem and professional confidence. This duality transforms social media into a double-edged sword—valuable for growth but equally capable of harming emotional well-being.

Consider the experience of a mid-career professional, Sarah, who navigates LinkedIn daily to stay informed and connected. One morning, she encounters a string of updates: a former colleague celebrating a promotion, another announcing their new position at a prestigious firm, and someone else sharing their Forbes recognition. Although she initially signed on to gain insights, Sarah leaves the platform feeling deflated. Instead of inspiration, she is left with the sinking feeling that she is falling behind. This is not an isolated experience. For countless professionals, social media shifts from being a tool for advancement to a mirror reflecting perceived inadequacies. It highlights a paradox: while these platforms were designed to foster connection, they often amplify feelings of isolation and doubt.

The issue stems from the inherent nature of social media, which thrives on the curation of content. On platforms like LinkedIn, users present carefully constructed narratives of their professional lives. Promotions, certifications, and achievements dominate the feed, while struggles, failures, and setbacks remain conspicuously absent. This selective sharing creates an illusion of effortless success, a highlight reel that contrasts starkly with the messy realities of work and life. It becomes easy to forget that every polished update represents a backstory filled with challenges that are rarely, if ever, shared.

The curated nature of these platforms would not be as impactful were it not for the innate human tendency toward social comparison. As psychologist Leon Festinger's social comparison theory suggests, people have a deep-seated need to evaluate themselves, often using others as benchmarks. When professionals like Sarah scroll through LinkedIn, they unconsciously compare their own journeys with the successes on display. This upward comparison—measuring oneself against those perceived to be better off—can erode self-esteem, especially when one's own achievements feel invisible or insufficient by comparison. As the line between aspiration and envy blurs, the promise of connection offered by social media turns into a source of professional insecurity.

While the professional value of platforms like LinkedIn is undeniable, their emotional toll is equally significant and often overlooked. Understanding this duality is essential to navigating the challenges they present. To do so requires more than simply reducing screen time; it demands a deeper awareness of how these platforms shape perceptions of success and self-worth. As we move through this chapter, we will explore the psychological mechanisms that drive professional envy and discuss strategies to mitigate its impact. Only by recognizing the double-edged nature of social media can professionals learn to wield it effectively, using it as a tool for growth rather than a source of lack of confidence.

THE PSYCHOLOGY OF PROFESSIONAL ENVY

Professional envy, though rarely discussed openly, is a deeply ingrained emotional response fueled by our intrinsic need to evaluate our standing relative to others. In the workplace, envy often stems from observing peers achieve milestones that seem unattainable or far removed from one's current position. When this dynamic extends into the digital realm—where social media platforms amplify curated narratives of success—the psychological impact becomes even more pronounced. Understanding the roots of professional envy requires unpacking the interplay between human psychology and the mechanics of social media.

Intrinsically, professional envy is a form of social comparison, a concept first articulated by psychologist Leon Festinger. According to his social comparison theory, individuals have an inherent drive to assess their abilities, achievements, and worth. When objective measures like performance reviews or promotions are absent, people turn to peers as benchmarks. On platforms like LinkedIn, the abundance of achievement-based content—promotions, awards, certifications—provides an endless stream of comparisons. These comparisons, particularly when focused on those perceived to be "above" oneself, often trigger feelings of inadequacy. Unlike the envy sparked by direct competitors in the workplace, social media amplifies this feeling by exposing users to a vast, global pool of highly curated success stories.

What differentiates professional envy in the social media age is its intensity and ubiquity. In face-to-face environments, envy is mitigated by context; we may witness a colleague's success but also see their struggles. On social media, this context is erased, replaced by a sanitized, idealized version of reality. Achievements appear effortless and linear, leading viewers to underestimate the challenges and failures behind the scenes. This distortion creates an emotional chasm between one's lived experiences and the imagined ease of others' accomplishments, exacerbating feelings of inadequacy and self-doubt.

The emotional impact of professional envy is multifaceted. At a surface level, it can manifest as dissatisfaction or frustration, but its deeper effects include diminished self-esteem and professional confidence. A professional who frequently encounters posts celebrating promotions or entrepreneurial milestones may begin questioning their own trajectory, doubting whether they are achieving enough or if their efforts are meaningful. Over time, these emotions can spiral into a persistent sense of professional stagnation, making it harder to recognize one's own progress or celebrate personal wins. The comparison trap becomes self-reinforcing: the more one views others' success stories, the more inadequate they feel, compelling them to seek validation through the same platforms, which only perpetuates the cycle.

Interestingly, professional envy is not entirely negative; it can have motivational effects when harnessed constructively. Psychologists distinguish between "malicious envy" and "benign envy." Malicious envy is destructive, fostering resentment and a desire to undermine others. In contrast, benign envy can spur self-improvement and goal-setting. For example, seeing a peer earn a certification might inspire someone to pursue further training or take proactive steps in their career. The challenge lies in recognizing and channeling envy in ways that promote growth rather than insecurity.

Understanding the psychology of professional envy is the first step toward managing its impact. By acknowledging that envy is a natural response rooted in human behavior, individuals can approach it with greater self-compassion. Furthermore, by reframing comparisons as opportunities for reflection and growth, professionals can transform envy from a source of discouragement into a catalyst for progress. The subsequent sections will delve into strategies for fostering this shift, empowering readers to navigate the complexities of social media without succumbing to its darker psychological effects.

THE UNIQUE IMPACT OF LINKEDIN

Among social media platforms, LinkedIn stands out for its professional focus, positioning itself as a space for career advancement, networking, and personal branding. While platforms like Instagram and Facebook might prompt lifestyle envy, LinkedIn uniquely fosters professional comparison, creating an ecosystem where users' successes, accolades, and opportunities are displayed in a highly curated, career-centric manner. This focus can amplify professional envy and self-criticism, making LinkedIn a double-edged sword for professionals seeking inspiration and growth.

One of LinkedIn's defining features is its emphasis on public recognition of achievements. Users share promotions, certifications, new jobs, and professional milestones—content that is designed to highlight their career trajectory in the most favorable light. For professionals scrolling through their feeds, this constant exposure to others' accomplishments can skew their perception of what is "normal" progress in a career. A single session on LinkedIn might present a flood of posts about new leadership roles, entrepreneurial ventures, or successful projects, giving the impression that everyone is moving forward at a rapid pace while their own progress stagnates. The platform's algorithm, designed to prioritize engagement, often amplifies such posts, further tilting the balance toward aspirational content.

LinkedIn's professional orientation also creates a unique pressure to measure up. Unlike other platforms, where sharing personal updates is optional, LinkedIn's very purpose encourages users to craft and maintain a public professional identity. This can lead to "performance anxiety" as individuals feel compelled to project a specific image of success, even if it does not align with their current reality. For example, someone struggling to find a job might feel pressured to share only positive updates, creating a disconnect between their online persona and their lived experience. This pressure to curate an idealized version of oneself can compound feelings of inadequacy and disconnection, especially when compared to the polished success stories of others.

The platform's design further reinforces the comparison trap. LinkedIn allows users to track their peers' career journeys in granular detail, from job titles to the timing of promotions. While this can be an excellent way to gain inspiration or understand industry trends, it also fosters unhealthy comparisons. Seeing a former classmate or colleague advance faster or into a seemingly more prestigious role can trigger self-doubt and questions about one's own choices. The public nature of LinkedIn endorsements and congratulatory posts—comments celebrating someone's achievements or milestones—can intensify these feelings, creating a sense of exclusion for those who feel they have little to share.

However, LinkedIn's impact is not uniformly negative. For those who approach the platform strategically, it can serve as a powerful tool for professional development. The key lies in how users interpret and interact with the content. When approached with a growth mindset, LinkedIn can inspire action, such as pursuing additional skills, networking proactively, or exploring new career paths. For example, rather than feeling defeated by a peer's certification announcement, a professional might view it as a prompt to evaluate their own goals and opportunities for growth. Additionally, LinkedIn's resources, including thought leadership articles and educational content, provide users with tangible ways to enhance their careers.

To mitigate the negative impact of LinkedIn, users must develop strategies to reframe their interactions with the platform. This includes recognizing that LinkedIn profiles often represent a highlight reel rather than a comprehensive view of someone's career. It's also essential to set boundaries around time spent on the platform and curate one's feed to prioritize content that aligns with personal goals and interests rather than triggering comparison. By shifting their focus from passive consumption to active engagement, users can reclaim LinkedIn as a space for genuine professional growth.

In essence, LinkedIn's unique impact lies in its ability to amplify both the opportunities and challenges of professional comparison. By understanding its dynamics and adopting intentional practices, professionals can navigate the platform in a way that enhances rather than detracts from their self-esteem and career development. The subsequent sections will explore practical strategies for redefining success and focusing on personal growth, offering actionable tools to counteract LinkedIn's comparison trap.

WHY PROFESSIONAL ENVY HURTS SELF-ESTEEM

Professional envy, while a natural human response, can be particularly corrosive to self-esteem when left unchecked. Unlike admiration, which can inspire growth, envy often carries a sense of inadequacy and resentment, leaving individuals focused more on what they lack than on their own achievements. In the professional context, where identity and self-worth are frequently tied to career success, this emotional response can have profound psychological and practical consequences.

One reason professional envy harms self-esteem is its tendency to distort perception. Envy often triggers a hyper-focus on others' achievements while minimizing or disregarding one's own. This cognitive bias leads individuals to overestimate the significance of someone else's success while underestimating the complexities or struggles that may have accompanied it. For example, seeing a colleague's promotion might evoke feelings of inferiority, even if the colleague's journey included challenges the observer is unaware of. This distorted view not only undermines self-confidence but also creates a false narrative of failure, reinforcing a sense of personal inadequacy.

Envy also erodes self-esteem by fostering unhealthy comparisons. In a competitive professional environment, individuals often benchmark their progress against peers, mentors, or even public figures. While comparisons can sometimes provide motivation, they often set unattainable standards that exacerbate feelings of deficiency. For instance, professionals who measure their career against someone with a vastly different background, skill set, or set of opportunities might feel they fall short, not because they lack ability, but because the comparison itself is inherently flawed. This relentless comparison amplifies self-questioning, making it harder to appreciate personal milestones or growth.

Another way professional envy undermines self-esteem is by encouraging avoidance behaviors. Instead of using envy as a signal to address areas for growth, individuals might retreat into inaction or procrastination out of fear of failure. The belief that they will never measure up to others can become a self-fulfilling prophecy, stifling ambition and preventing them from pursuing new challenges. For example, someone envious of a colleague's public speaking skills might avoid presenting at meetings, reinforcing the idea that they are less capable. Over time, this avoidance not only limits opportunities but also diminishes self-worth, as individuals begin to internalize their perceived shortcomings.

Furthermore, the emotional toll of professional envy can lead to a cycle of negative self-talk and self-criticism. Envy often whispers harmful internal narratives: "Why haven't I achieved that yet?" or "I'm just not good enough." This internal dialogue becomes a persistent drain on self-esteem, creating a loop where feelings of inadequacy fuel further envy, and envy, in turn, deepens the sense of inadequacy. Such a cycle can become particularly damaging in high-pressure environments, where external validation is often prioritized over internal fulfillment.

However, the harm caused by professional envy is not irreversible. Recognizing and addressing envy as a natural but manageable emotion is the first step toward mitigating its impact on self-esteem. Reframing envy as an opportunity to identify personal goals can transform it into a constructive force. For example, instead of feeling defeated by a peer's success, individuals can use their envy as a prompt to reflect on their own aspirations and consider actionable steps to achieve them. This shift in mindset not only breaks the cycle of self-criticism but also fosters a sense of agency and empowerment.

Moreover, cultivating self-compassion can counterbalance the negative effects of professional envy. By acknowledging that everyone's career journey is unique and filled with its own challenges, individuals can reduce the pressure to compete or compare. Practices such as mindfulness and gratitude can help professionals focus on their strengths and accomplishments, reinforcing a more balanced and resilient sense of self-worth.

In essence, professional envy hurts self-esteem by distorting perceptions, fostering harmful comparisons, and perpetuating self-critical narratives. Yet, with self-awareness and intentional strategies, it is possible to transform envy from a source of pain into a catalyst for growth. By recognizing envy's impact and adopting healthier responses, individuals can protect their self-esteem and cultivate a more grounded sense of professional identity.

MANAGING THE IMPACT: PRACTICAL STRATEGIES

Overcoming the negative effects of professional envy requires more than awareness—it demands deliberate action and a shift in perspective. While it is impossible to entirely avoid feelings of envy, individuals can adopt strategies to mitigate its impact on their self-esteem and career satisfaction. By cultivating healthier habits and mindsets, professionals can transform envy from a paralyzing force into a catalyst for growth and motivation.

One of the most effective strategies for managing professional envy is reframing one's perspective through self-reflection. Instead of viewing another person's success as a threat, it can be seen as evidence of what is possible. This shift requires asking constructive questions: "What can I learn from their journey?" or "How does this achievement align with my aspirations?" For example, observing a colleague's career milestone might inspire a reassessment of one's own goals and a recommitment to long-term ambitions. Through intentional reflection, envy becomes a source of insight rather than insecurity, fostering a growth-oriented mindset.

Setting boundaries with social media and other professional platforms is another essential strategy. LinkedIn, for instance, often curates a highlight reel of achievements that can intensify feelings of inadequacy. Limiting exposure to these platforms or curating one's feed to prioritize meaningful content can reduce the emotional toll. Instead of passively scrolling, individuals might engage more actively by celebrating others' successes or sharing their own professional milestones. This shift from comparison to connection fosters a sense of community and reinforces the idea that success is not a zero-sum game.

Practicing gratitude can also be a powerful antidote to envy. When focused on what others have, it is easy to overlook personal accomplishments and strengths. Keeping a daily or weekly gratitude journal that highlights professional achievements—no matter how small—can help individuals anchor their self-worth in their own progress. For instance, reflecting on a completed project, a kind word from a colleague, or a skill improvement can remind individuals of their value and uniqueness. Over time, this habit shifts attention from external validation to internal fulfillment, reducing the grip of envy on one's self-esteem.

Building and nurturing authentic professional relationships is another way to manage the impact of envy. Open conversations with peers, mentors, or colleagues about challenges and successes can demystify others' achievements and reveal the struggles behind their victories. For example, a colleague who seems effortlessly successful may share stories of setbacks and persistence, providing a more nuanced and relatable perspective. Such connections foster empathy and collaboration, turning potential sources of envy into opportunities for mutual support and learning.

Lastly, goal-setting and personal development are vital tools for countering envy's effects. Often, envy arises from a sense of stagnation or lack of direction. By setting clear, actionable goals, individuals can channel the energy behind envy into constructive efforts. For instance, identifying specific skills to develop or milestones to achieve creates a sense of purpose and progress. Breaking these goals into manageable steps ensures steady advancement, reducing the tendency to fixate on others' accomplishments.

Importantly, these strategies are not about suppressing envy but rather about transforming it into a force for good. Acknowledging envy as a natural response allows individuals to confront it with compassion rather than shame. By combining self-awareness with intentional practices, professionals can reclaim their sense of agency, fostering confidence and resilience in the face of challenges.

Managing the impact of professional envy is an ongoing process that requires effort and patience. Yet, by reframing perspectives, setting boundaries, practicing gratitude, building connections, and pursuing personal growth, individuals can protect their self-esteem and thrive in their professional lives. In doing so, they not only mitigate the harm caused by envy but also cultivate a more fulfilling and balanced career trajectory.

CASE STUDIES AND SUCCESS STORIES

Real-world examples provide a tangible lens through which to understand and navigate professional envy. Stories of individuals who have transformed feelings of inadequacy into personal growth illustrate the power of intentional effort and mindset shifts. These narratives not only offer practical insights but also inspire hope, showing that it is possible to rise above the challenges posed by professional envy and emerge stronger.

Case Study: Transforming Envy into Inspiration

Sarah, a marketing professional in her mid-30s, frequently found herself envious of her peers on LinkedIn. She noticed a former colleague, Rachel, repeatedly posting about high-profile campaigns and awards. Each update made Sarah question her own career choices, leaving her feeling stagnant and undervalued.

Instead of succumbing to despair, Sarah decided to analyze Rachel's success objectively. She reached out to Rachel for a casual coffee meeting, framing it as a chance to reconnect and learn.

During their conversation, Sarah discovered that Rachel's achievements stemmed not from luck but from consistent networking and targeted skill development. Inspired, Sarah reflected on her own career goals and identified areas for improvement. She enrolled in an online course on digital marketing trends and began building relationships within her industry. A year later, Sarah secured a leadership role in her company, directly attributing her success to the proactive steps she had taken. By confronting her envy and seeking inspiration, Sarah turned a potential source of distress into a transformative opportunity.

Case Study: Overcoming the Illusion of Perfection

James, an entry-level software engineer, struggled with professional envy when scrolling through his LinkedIn feed. He frequently compared himself to his university classmate, Alex, who had secured a coveted position at a renowned tech firm. James assumed Alex's career trajectory was flawless, leading him to question his own capabilities. However, during a chance encounter at a networking event, James mustered the courage to ask Alex about his experiences.

To James's surprise, Alex candidly shared the pressures and challenges of his high-profile job, including frequent late nights and the emotional toll of imposter syndrome. This conversation helped James realize that success is often accompanied by unseen struggles. James shifted his focus toward honing his technical skills and contributing meaningfully to his current role. Within two years, he earned recognition at his company for his innovative projects and was promoted to a managerial position. James's ability to humanize Alex's achievements and focus on his own path was instrumental in overcoming his feelings of inadequacy.

Success Story: Building Confidence Through Connection

Priya, a mid-career HR professional, often felt inadequate compared to her peers who frequently posted about promotions and certifications. Feeling isolated, she decided to join a local professional development group to expand her network. Through this group, Priya connected with mentors and peers who shared their experiences and provided constructive feedback.

One mentor advised her to focus on her unique strengths and align her goals with her values. Taking this advice to heart, Priya implemented new initiatives at her workplace to improve employee engagement, a passion she had always nurtured. Her efforts earned her recognition within her organization, and she was eventually invited to speak at an industry conference. Priya's success came not from trying to match others' accomplishments but from leveraging her unique talents and building meaningful connections.

Success Story: Redefining Success on Personal Terms

Ethan, a freelance graphic designer, often compared himself to other designers on Instagram who showcased seemingly endless streams of high-profile clients and polished projects. This comparison eroded his self-esteem, making him feel that his work was inadequate. However, after attending a workshop on mindfulness and creativity, Ethan began reassessing what success meant to him.

He realized his primary motivation was creative freedom and the ability to balance work with personal time. Ethan started sharing his design process on Instagram, focusing on authenticity rather than perfection. His posts attracted a niche audience that valued his transparency and unique style. Over time, Ethan built a loyal client base that appreciated his approach, allowing him to thrive without chasing superficial markers of success.

These case studies and success stories underscore the transformative potential of addressing professional envy head-on. By seeking connection, redefining success, and focusing on personal growth, individuals can shift their perspective, overcome insecurity, and unlock new opportunities. These examples serve as a reminder that envy, while challenging, can ultimately fuel positive change when approached with intention and resilience.

Redefining Success

The concept of success has long been tied to visible, external markers—wealth, titles, awards, and public recognition. From an early age, individuals are conditioned to aspire to a specific version of achievement, often shaped by societal expectations, cultural norms, and professional environments. Whether it's earning a degree from a prestigious university, landing a high-paying job, or climbing the corporate ladder, these benchmarks are heralded as the epitome of accomplishment. Yet, while these goals can be meaningful for some, they often fail to capture the diverse and nuanced aspirations that make life fulfilling.

Traditional success narratives are deeply ingrained in professional culture. Platforms like LinkedIn amplify these standards by celebrating promotions, accolades, and milestones in highly visible ways. This visibility creates a perception that success is linear and universally defined, with little room for deviation. As a result, individuals may feel compelled to conform, fearing that any divergence from this path signals failure. Over time, this rigid framework can lead to feelings of inadequacy and dissatisfaction, as achievements become less about personal fulfillment and more about meeting external expectations.

The pitfalls of this narrative are not new. Philosophers, psychologists, and social scientists have long critiqued the pursuit of external validation as a fragile and often unsatisfying foundation for happiness. For instance, philosopher Alain de Botton highlights the concept of "status anxiety," wherein people become trapped in a relentless comparison cycle, measuring their worth against others' achievements. Similarly, studies in positive psychology have shown that external rewards, while initially gratifying, have diminishing returns over time. When success is measured solely by others' standards, it becomes a moving target—always just out of reach.

This chapter aims to challenge the traditional success narrative, encouraging individuals to examine its limitations and rethink its relevance to their lives. By understanding how these societal expectations shape their professional ambitions, readers can begin to dismantle harmful patterns and replace them with a more personalized, fulfilling approach to success. Redefining success is not about rejecting ambition but about aligning it with one's values and aspirations. Only then can individuals cultivate a sense of purpose and satisfaction that transcends fleeting applause or arbitrary benchmarks.

THE ROLE OF INTRINSIC VS. EXTRINSIC MOTIVATION IN SUCCESS

Success, as commonly understood, is often driven by extrinsic motivators— external rewards such as money, recognition, and status. These tangible incentives hold undeniable appeal, providing a sense of validation and achievement. However, extrinsic motivation, while powerful, tends to be short-lived, its effects fading as the initial thrill of accomplishment wanes. In contrast, intrinsic motivation—rooted in personal values, interests, and the joy of the process itself—offers a more sustainable path to fulfillment. Understanding the interplay between these two forces is essential to redefining success in a way that fosters lasting satisfaction and growth.

Extrinsic motivators are deeply embedded in societal and professional structures. Promotions, bonuses, and awards are celebrated milestones that reinforce the idea that success is primarily about external validation. This framework is not without merit; extrinsic rewards can inspire effort and discipline, especially in the face of challenging tasks. However, overreliance on such rewards can lead to a hollow pursuit where individuals prioritize appearances over substance. Research in psychology, such as Edward Deci and Richard Ryan's self-determination theory, highlights that extrinsic motivation alone can undermine long-term engagement and well-being, particularly when it overshadows intrinsic motivators.

In contrast, intrinsic motivation arises from internal drives such as curiosity, passion, and the desire for mastery. It is fueled by the satisfaction of pursuing meaningful goals rather than the promise of external rewards. Intrinsic motivation fosters resilience, creativity, and sustained effort, as individuals are more likely to persevere in activities that align with their personal interests and values. For example, an artist painting for the love of creation, or a professional seeking to solve a challenging problem out of intellectual curiosity, experiences a deeper sense of accomplishment than someone pursuing these activities solely for external recognition.

The balance between intrinsic and extrinsic motivation varies among individuals and circumstances, but a dominance of extrinsic drivers often leads to burnout and dissatisfaction. In the workplace, for instance, professionals may chase promotions or high-paying roles without questioning whether these align with their personal goals or interests. Over time, this misalignment erodes their intrinsic motivation, turning work into a means to an end rather than a source of fulfillment. Studies show that individuals who pursue intrinsically motivated goals—those tied to personal growth, relationships, or societal contribution—report higher levels of happiness and life satisfaction compared to those driven primarily by extrinsic factors.

Redefining success requires a shift in focus from extrinsic to intrinsic motivation. This does not mean disregarding external achievements but placing greater value on the inner rewards of growth, learning, and self-expression. By identifying what truly matters on a personal level, individuals can chart a path to success that feels authentic and enriching. Ultimately, success becomes less about impressing others and more about fulfilling one's own potential and aspirations.

PERSONALIZING THE DEFINITION OF SUCCESS

The concept of success is often presented as a one-size-fits-all formula—wealth, status, and power being the quintessential markers. However, this traditional framework overlooks a fundamental truth: success is deeply personal and varies widely across individuals. Defining success in a way that aligns with one's values, passions, and circumstances is essential for achieving a sense of fulfillment and purpose. Personalizing the definition of success is not merely a philosophical exercise but a practical strategy for reclaiming agency in a world dominated by external pressures.

Many individuals inherit their definition of success from societal expectations, familial influences, or cultural norms. These external sources often dictate what goals are worth pursuing, such as earning a specific income, attaining a prestigious job title, or achieving a certain lifestyle. While these benchmarks can provide structure and motivation, they frequently lead to dissatisfaction if they do not resonate with an individual's personal desires. For instance, someone who prioritizes family and community over financial ambition might find a high-stakes corporate career unfulfilling, even if it checks every box on the societal success checklist.

Personalizing success begins with introspection. Identifying core values, passions, and priorities requires honest reflection and a willingness to question conventional wisdom. Tools such as journaling, vision boards, or guided exercises in self-assessment can help clarify what matters most. For example, a professional might discover that they derive the greatest satisfaction from mentoring others rather than climbing the corporate ladder. Similarly, an entrepreneur might realize that fostering innovation and creativity outweighs the pursuit of rapid financial gains. By aligning goals with intrinsic values, individuals create a definition of success that feels authentic and meaningful.

Another critical aspect of personalizing success is acknowledging that it is dynamic, not static. Life circumstances, experiences, and priorities evolve over time, necessitating periodic reassessment of what success means. A young professional might initially focus on career advancement but later prioritize work-life balance or social impact as they grow older. Viewing success as an adaptable concept allows individuals to remain true to themselves while navigating different stages of life. This flexibility prevents stagnation and ensures that success continues to be a source of fulfillment rather than frustration.

Personalizing the definition of success empowers individuals to break free from societal comparisons and external validation. It shifts the focus from living up to others' expectations to pursuing a life that is uniquely fulfilling. This redefinition transforms success from a destination to a journey—one marked by alignment with one's authentic self and the pursuit of goals that genuinely inspire. In doing so, individuals cultivate a deeper sense of purpose and resilience, enabling them to thrive on their own terms.

BENEFITS OF FOCUSING ON PERSONAL GROWTH

Shifting the focus from external validation to personal growth is a transformative approach to success that yields profound and multifaceted benefits. While traditional markers of success, such as promotions, accolades, or financial milestones, are tangible and visible, they often come at the cost of personal well-being and satisfaction. Conversely, prioritizing personal growth fosters resilience, creativity, and long-term fulfillment, enabling individuals to thrive in both their personal and professional lives.

One of the most significant benefits of focusing on personal growth is the cultivation of self-awareness. When individuals prioritize growth, they actively engage in self-reflection, exploring their strengths, weaknesses, values, and aspirations. This deepened self-understanding allows them to make more intentional decisions, pursue meaningful goals, and recognize their unique potential. For example, an employee who focuses on developing leadership skills not only enhances their career prospects but also gains confidence and clarity about their role in a team. This awareness reduces reliance on external approval, empowering individuals to measure success by their own progress rather than societal benchmarks.

Another advantage of personal growth is its ability to build resilience in the face of challenges. Unlike external achievements, which are often fragile and dependent on external factors, personal growth creates an internal foundation of strength. For instance, someone who works on improving their emotional intelligence and stress-management skills is better equipped to navigate workplace conflicts or personal setbacks. This resilience not only helps individuals recover from failures but also enables them to view obstacles as opportunities for learning. By adopting a growth mindset, they develop a sense of adaptability that is crucial in today's rapidly changing world.

Focusing on personal growth also fosters intrinsic motivation, which is more sustainable than the fleeting satisfaction derived from external rewards. When individuals pursue goals that align with their passions and values, they experience a sense of purpose that fuels long-term commitment and effort. For example, a professional who chooses to deepen their expertise in a field they love is likely to find the journey itself rewarding, regardless of recognition or external rewards. This intrinsic motivation enhances productivity, creativity, and overall satisfaction, as individuals find joy in the process rather than fixating solely on outcomes.

Lastly, personal growth enhances relationships by encouraging empathy, communication, and collaboration. As individuals work on understanding themselves, they also become more attuned to the needs and perspectives of others. This awareness fosters stronger connections, both personally and professionally. For instance, a manager who prioritizes personal development in areas like active listening and conflict resolution creates a more inclusive and supportive workplace culture. These improved relationships contribute to a sense of belonging and mutual respect, which are essential for holistic success.

In focusing on personal growth, individuals shift from chasing external validation to nurturing their inner potential. This approach not only brings long-lasting fulfillment but also equips them with the tools to navigate life's complexities with confidence and grace. By investing in growth, individuals not only enhance their own well-being but also inspire and positively impact those around them, creating a ripple effect of progress and empowerment.

OVERCOMING THE PRESSURE OF EXTERNAL VALIDATION

The pressure to seek external validation is a pervasive challenge in professional and personal lives. It is fueled by societal norms, corporate cultures, and social media's curated portrayals of success. Many individuals measure their worth by external markers, such as job titles, salary brackets, or peer recognition, often sacrificing authenticity and mental well-being. Overcoming this pressure is not merely about rejecting external opinions but about reframing one's relationship with validation to cultivate a healthier and more sustainable approach to success.

One critical step in overcoming the need for external validation is recognizing its roots. Many individuals grow up in environments where approval is tied to achievement. Whether through grades in school, praise for extracurricular success, or comparisons with siblings and peers, the message often becomes clear: worthiness is conditional. In adulthood, these ingrained patterns manifest as a relentless pursuit of recognition, whether through promotions or public accolades. Understanding this psychological foundation can empower individuals to question why they seek external approval and to distinguish between genuine aspirations and inherited expectations.

Another essential strategy is fostering self-compassion. Many people rely on external validation as a way to counteract their internal self-criticism. They believe that achievements will silence their doubts or prove their worth. However, research shows that self-compassion is far more effective in promoting resilience and self-worth. When individuals treat themselves with kindness, particularly in moments of failure or inadequacy, they reduce the need to seek external reassurance. Instead of striving for perfection, they can focus on growth and effort, creating a more balanced and fulfilling approach to personal and professional development.

Setting boundaries around external influences is also key. Social media platforms and workplace cultures can amplify the pressure to conform to external standards of success. For example, an employee may feel compelled to work long hours or prioritize visibility over meaningful contributions because of organizational norms. To counter this, individuals can establish clear boundaries that protect their mental and emotional well-being. This might involve limiting time on platforms like LinkedIn, where professional comparisons are rampant, or practicing assertiveness to resist pressures to conform. By creating these boundaries, individuals reclaim control over their definitions of success.

Lastly, embracing intrinsic motivation as the primary driver of success can fundamentally shift the dynamic. Intrinsic motivation, rooted in personal values and passions, helps individuals align their actions with their authentic selves. For instance, a professional who finds meaning in mentoring colleagues may prioritize this role over external rewards like awards or recognition. By focusing on what genuinely matters to them, individuals not only experience greater satisfaction but also reduce the anxiety associated with external judgments. This alignment between actions and values fosters a sense of integrity and purpose, making external validation less relevant.

Overcoming the pressure of external validation is an ongoing journey that requires self-awareness, intentionality, and resilience. By understanding its origins, practicing self-compassion, setting boundaries, and prioritizing intrinsic motivation, individuals can liberate themselves from the cycle of seeking approval. In doing so, they create space for authentic growth and fulfillment, redefining success on their own terms and finding confidence in their unique paths.

PRACTICAL STRATEGIES FOR REDEFINING SUCCESS

Redefining success is not merely an abstract exercise; it requires actionable steps that empower individuals to shift their focus from external metrics to personal growth and fulfillment. While societal and cultural pressures may promote traditional measures of achievement, such as financial wealth or social status, practical strategies can help individuals align their definitions of success with their values, passions, and intrinsic motivations. This process involves introspection, intentional goal-setting, and the cultivation of habits that support a more authentic and satisfying life trajectory.

The first strategy is to conduct a personal success audit. This involves reflecting on past accomplishments and evaluating whether they brought genuine satisfaction or were driven primarily by external expectations. For example, someone might consider a time when they pursued a promotion solely for its prestige, only to feel unfulfilled afterward. This exercise helps individuals identify patterns and distinguish between achievements that aligned with their values and those that didn't. Journaling can be a helpful tool during this process, as it allows individuals to articulate their thoughts and uncover deeper motivations.

Goal-setting is another essential practice for redefining success. Traditional goals often emphasize outcomes, such as earning a specific salary or attaining a particular position. Instead, individuals can focus on process-oriented goals that reflect personal growth and well-being. For instance, instead of aiming to become a manager by a certain age, a person might set a goal to enhance their leadership skills or build stronger relationships with colleagues. These types of goals encourage continuous improvement and provide a sense of accomplishment, even if external benchmarks remain unmet.

Building a community of like-minded individuals is also critical. Surrounding oneself with people who prioritize personal growth over external validation creates a supportive environment that reinforces healthier definitions of success. These communities can take various forms, such as mentorship networks, professional groups, or even close friendships. By engaging with others who value authenticity and intrinsic motivation, individuals are less likely to succumb to societal pressures or compare themselves to those pursuing traditional markers of success.

Another powerful strategy is practicing gratitude and mindfulness. These habits shift the focus from what is lacking to what is already present, reducing the tendency to seek validation from external sources. Regular gratitude exercises, such as listing three things one appreciates each day, can foster a mindset of abundance rather than scarcity. Mindfulness practices, such as meditation, help individuals stay grounded in the present moment, enabling them to recognize and appreciate their progress without constantly striving for external approval.

Finally, embracing failure as a learning opportunity can redefine how success is perceived. Many people view setbacks as evidence of inadequacy, reinforcing the need for external validation to restore their sense of worth. However, reframing failure as an integral part of growth transforms these experiences into valuable lessons. For example, a rejected proposal at work can be seen as a chance to refine ideas and improve communication skills. By focusing on what can be learned rather than what was lost, individuals cultivate resilience and a growth mindset that supports long-term success.

Redefining success is a dynamic and ongoing process, but these practical strategies provide a solid foundation. By conducting personal audits, setting meaningful goals, fostering supportive communities, practicing gratitude and mindfulness, and embracing failure, individuals can shift their focus from external validation to personal growth. In doing so, they create a life defined not by societal expectations but by their unique aspirations and values. This redefinition paves the way for a more fulfilling and self-directed journey.

Real-world examples illuminate the transformative power of redefining success, showcasing how individuals across different contexts have shifted their focus from external validation to personal growth. These case studies demonstrate the challenges and rewards of breaking away from traditional success narratives, offering inspiration and practical lessons for readers.

Case Study 1: From Corporate Climber to Purpose-Driven Entrepreneur

Samantha, a mid-career professional, spent over a decade climbing the corporate ladder, driven by the allure of promotions, bonuses, and accolades. Despite her achievements, she often felt unfulfilled and disconnected from her work. After attending a leadership retreat, Samantha realized her values centered on creativity and impact rather than hierarchical advancement.

She left her corporate role to start a small business designing sustainable fashion. Initially, the transition was fraught with doubts and financial uncertainties. However, by focusing on her intrinsic motivation to create and contribute to environmental sustainability, Samantha found deep satisfaction. Her definition of success shifted from external validation, such as industry awards, to the joy of creating products aligned with her values. Today, she considers her small but meaningful contribution to sustainable living a far greater accomplishment than her corporate titles ever were.

Case Study 2: Redefining Academic Achievement

James, a university student, struggled with the pressure to excel academically, viewing high grades as the ultimate marker of success. This mindset left him anxious and unable to enjoy the learning process. After attending a workshop on growth mindset principles, James began to approach his studies differently.

Instead of obsessing over grades, he focused on mastering subjects that genuinely interested him, such as environmental policy. He also sought mentorship opportunities and engaged in research projects that aligned with his passions. Though his GPA remained solid rather than stellar, James developed a sense of purpose and confidence in his abilities. He now works as a policy analyst, where his expertise and passion are valued far more than the grades he once thought defined him.

Case Study 3: A Personal Journey in Overcoming Comparison

Maria, a software engineer, often felt inadequate when comparing herself to peers on LinkedIn who frequently posted about promotions, new projects, or certifications. Her self-esteem took a hit, and she began doubting her career progress. A coach suggested Maria identify her personal goals and disconnect from social media temporarily.

During her hiatus, Maria discovered her passion for mentoring junior developers and contributing to open-source projects. She set personal benchmarks that reflected these priorities, such as helping five mentees advance in their careers and contributing to three open-source initiatives annually. When she returned to social media, she used it to share knowledge rather than seek approval. This reframing allowed her to feel successful based on her unique contributions rather than external comparisons.

Case Study 4: A Team Redefining Success Together

A marketing team at a mid-sized firm faced high turnover due to relentless pressure to outperform competitors and achieve quarterly targets. The team's new manager, Raj, decided to redefine what success meant for the group. Instead of focusing solely on revenue metrics, Raj emphasized creativity, collaboration, and long-term client relationships.

He introduced initiatives like "Innovation Fridays," where team members could brainstorm freely, and monthly sessions to share lessons from both successes and failures. Over time, morale improved, turnover decreased, and the team's work began to stand out for its originality and authenticity. By aligning their goals with personal and professional growth, the team achieved sustainable success that extended beyond short-term metrics.

Example: A Leader's Perspective on Redefining Success

Emily, the CEO of a nonprofit organization, once believed that success was measured by the number of awards her organization received and the size of its donor base. However, when a key initiative failed to deliver expected results, she began questioning this definition.

Through introspection and feedback from her team, Emily shifted her focus to impact rather than accolades. She restructured her organization to prioritize measurable outcomes for the communities they served, even if it meant taking on fewer high-profile projects. This approach not only improved the nonprofit's effectiveness but also deepened Emily's sense of fulfillment, as she felt her work truly aligned with her mission.

These case studies and examples illustrate the diverse ways individuals and teams can redefine success, moving away from societal expectations and external validation toward a focus on personal growth and authentic achievement. By doing so, they unlock greater satisfaction, resilience, and meaning in their pursuits. These stories remind readers that success is not one-size-fits-all but a deeply personal journey shaped by values, aspirations, and choices.

EMPOWERING TO EMBRACE AUTHENTIC SUCCESS

The journey to redefine success begins with recognizing that true achievement comes from alignment with one's values, aspirations, and inner growth. Empowering readers to embrace authentic success requires providing tools, perspectives, and encouragement that help them move away from societal expectations and toward a more fulfilling, personalized vision of success. This shift is not merely philosophical—it's transformative, offering a deeper sense of purpose and lasting contentment.

Recognizing Individuality in Success

Every person's definition of success is as unique as their fingerprint, shaped by their experiences, priorities, and dreams. Yet societal norms often attempt to homogenize success, presenting it as a checklist of wealth, titles, and accolades. Empowering readers starts with affirming that their aspirations may—and should—differ from conventional ideals.

Consider the analogy of climbing a mountain. For some, success might mean reaching the peak of their industry, while for others, it could mean enjoying the journey, contributing to their community, or simply choosing a different mountain to climb. By validating diverse definitions of success, readers can begin to release themselves from the pressure of conforming to external standards and embrace what genuinely matters to them.

Cultivating Self-Awareness

Self-awareness is the cornerstone of authentic success. It begins with introspection: What motivates me? What brings me joy? What values do I hold most dear? Without this clarity, it's easy to chase goals that feel empty once achieved. Empowering readers involves encouraging them to reflect on their personal and professional lives, identifying what aligns with their core values.

Journaling, meditation, and values-mapping exercises can help readers uncover their intrinsic drivers. These practices allow them to connect with their authentic selves and distinguish between goals they truly desire and those imposed by external pressures. With this insight, individuals are better equipped to set meaningful objectives that resonate with their inner values.

Building the Courage to Diverge

Redefining success often requires stepping away from the status quo, which can be intimidating. Readers may fear judgment, failure, or uncertainty when choosing an unconventional path. Empowerment lies in fostering resilience and self-confidence, equipping readers to embrace their choices even in the face of doubt or criticism.

Stories of trailblazers who defied societal norms to pursue their passions can serve as powerful sources of inspiration. For instance, individuals who left lucrative careers to follow creative or philanthropic endeavors demonstrate that the courage to diverge can lead to deeply fulfilling outcomes. These examples remind readers that while the path to authentic success may not always be smooth, it is ultimately rewarding.

Creating a Framework for Personal Success

Empowerment becomes actionable when readers are given a framework to design their unique success journey. This framework involves setting goals, measuring progress, and celebrating milestones aligned with personal growth rather than societal benchmarks.

1. **Set Personal Goals:** Readers are encouraged to identify specific, value-driven goals. These might include learning a new skill, building stronger relationships, or contributing to a cause they care about.

2. **Measure What Matters:** Instead of focusing on external rewards, readers can track their progress through metrics like skill mastery, emotional well-being, or impact on others.

3. **Celebrate Small Wins:** Empower readers to acknowledge and appreciate their achievements, no matter how small. This practice reinforces the mindset that every step forward is meaningful.

Finding Community and Support

Empowerment is amplified through connection. Readers may find strength in surrounding themselves with like-minded individuals who share their commitment to personal growth and authentic success. Support networks—whether friends, mentors, or online communities—offer encouragement, perspective, and shared wisdom.

Readers can also benefit from seeking role models who embody their ideal of success. Observing how these individuals navigate their journeys provides practical insights and reassurance that it's possible to succeed on one's terms.

Empowerment Through Reflection

Finally, individuals are encouraged to reflect regularly on their evolving definitions of success. Life circumstances and priorities change, and with them, the meaning of success may shift. By periodically revisiting their goals and values, readers ensure that their pursuit of success remains dynamic and aligned with their true selves.

Chapter 6: Building Resilience Against Rejection

Failure is often treated as a mark of inadequacy, a signal that one's efforts, abilities, or worth fell short. In professional settings, this perception can be especially harsh, with rejection sometimes feeling like a permanent stain on one's career aspirations. Whether it's a missed promotion, a declined job application, or a poorly received project, rejection tends to carry an emotional weight that lingers. The experience can evoke feelings of shame, embarrassment, and self-doubt, as individuals wrestle with internal questions about their competence and future prospects. In this environment, failure becomes something to fear and avoid at all costs, breeding anxiety and hesitation.

This response to failure is not without its roots in societal norms and cultural narratives. Success stories often highlight the end results while glossing over the setbacks along the way, reinforcing the idea that triumph should come swiftly and without error. This skewed portrayal fosters unrealistic expectations, making individuals more likely to see their own failures as personal deficiencies rather than inevitable parts of growth. Compounding the issue, many workplaces emphasize metrics, results, and performance without openly acknowledging the learning curve that failure can necessitate. In such settings, rejection is easily misconstrued as evidence of weakness, further solidifying its negative perception.

However, the perception of failure as inherently negative is not universal. In some cultures and industries, failure is reframed as an essential step toward innovation and discovery. Entrepreneurs and creators, for example, often celebrate their missteps as lessons that inform future success. This mindset is less about minimizing the pain of rejection and more about recognizing its utility. By reshaping the narrative, failure transforms from a dead-end into a pivot point—a redirection toward new approaches, insights, and opportunities. For individuals stuck in the cycle of self-recrimination, this alternative perspective can serve as a powerful tool for change.

The first step in reframing failure is understanding that rejection is not a reflection of one's inherent value but a momentary event shaped by circumstances. It is an experience shared by virtually everyone, from the most seasoned professionals to those just starting their careers. By normalizing failure and shedding the stigma attached to it, individuals can begin to approach rejection with curiosity rather than fear. This chapter aims to guide readers through that transformation, starting with an honest exploration of failure's emotional impact and moving toward practical strategies for growth.

UNDERSTANDING THE PSYCHOLOGY OF REJECTION

Rejection is more than a simple disappointment; it triggers a cascade of psychological responses that often feel disproportionate to the event itself. Research in neuroscience has revealed that social rejection activates the same regions of the brain as physical pain, underscoring the profound impact it can have on an individual's emotional state. This overlap, first highlighted in studies like those by Naomi Eisenberger, helps explain why being turned down for a promotion or losing a client can feel not just disheartening but genuinely wounding. The pain is real, even if it is intangible, and it often prompts people to adopt defensive behaviors to avoid further exposure to such vulnerability.

Compounding this emotional response are the cognitive distortions that often accompany rejection. Many individuals fall prey to patterns of catastrophizing or overgeneralization, interpreting one setback as evidence of widespread failure. A missed opportunity might lead to thoughts like, "I'll never succeed," or, "I'm just not good enough," which distort reality and deepen feelings of inadequacy. These internal narratives are often fueled by past experiences, such as childhood criticism or prior professional failures, that create entrenched beliefs about one's worth or abilities. Over time, these distortions can lead to a cycle of avoidance, where the fear of rejection prevents individuals from taking risks or pursuing opportunities that could lead to success.

Another important factor in the psychology of rejection is the role of social comparison. In professional environments, where achievements are often visible and celebrated, it's easy to measure oneself against peers. This dynamic is particularly evident in the age of LinkedIn and other social platforms, where curated success stories dominate. When individuals encounter rejection, they may contrast their own struggles with the apparent ease of others' accomplishments, further eroding their confidence. This comparison, while often inaccurate, can feel inescapable, amplifying the emotional toll of rejection and reinforcing the belief that they are falling behind.

Understanding these psychological mechanisms is crucial because it demystifies the intense reactions rejection often provokes. Recognizing that these responses are rooted in biology and learned behaviors allows individuals to approach rejection with greater compassion for themselves. It is not a personal failing to feel hurt by rejection; it is a deeply human reaction. By acknowledging this, people can begin to break free from the cycle of self-criticism and instead focus on strategies for resilience. This shift requires reframing rejection not as a measure of worth but as a stepping stone toward growth, an idea that will be explored in depth in the following sections.

WHY FAILURE IS VALUABLE

Failure, though often unwelcome, is one of life's most potent teachers. At its core, failure provides feedback—clear, unfiltered information about what doesn't work. Unlike success, which can sometimes obscure underlying issues, failure forces individuals to confront weaknesses, gaps in knowledge, or misaligned strategies. This clarity is invaluable. It illuminates paths for improvement, whether by refining a skill, adjusting a process, or rethinking an approach. Viewed through this lens, failure becomes less a verdict on one's abilities and more a source of insight that fuels long-term growth.

Beyond providing feedback, failure cultivates resilience. Each instance of rejection or setback tests an individual's capacity to recover and adapt. Resilience is not a fixed trait but a skill honed through repeated exposure to adversity. Professionals who embrace their failures learn how to navigate uncertainty, regulate their emotions, and maintain focus despite challenges. Over time, this ability to persevere creates a robust inner strength that becomes a critical asset in both professional and personal contexts. Far from being a liability, the experience of failure builds a psychological foundation that supports sustained achievement.

Moreover, failure fosters creativity and innovation. In industries where progress relies on experimentation—such as technology, science, and the arts—failure is not just an occasional occurrence; it is an expectation. The willingness to fail encourages bold thinking and risk-taking, pushing boundaries that would otherwise remain untested. Historical examples abound, from Thomas Edison's iterative journey to invent the light bulb to modern entrepreneurs who pivot their business models after initial missteps. These stories underscore that failure often precedes groundbreaking success, serving as a catalyst for fresh ideas and unconventional solutions.

Finally, failure nurtures humility and empathy—qualities that enhance professional relationships and leadership effectiveness. Experiencing rejection firsthand provides a deeper understanding of the struggles others face, fostering a sense of connection and compassion. Leaders who have encountered failure often demonstrate greater emotional intelligence, as they can relate to their teams' challenges and provide support grounded in shared experience. This ability to connect authentically can transform workplaces, creating environments where failure is not feared but embraced as part of the collective journey toward improvement.

Failure's value lies not in the pain it brings but in what it offers afterward: insight, resilience, innovation, and connection. By reframing failure as a necessary and even beneficial part of growth, individuals can begin to see rejection not as an end, but as a momentary obstacle on the path to something greater.

EXAMPLES OF RESILIENCE FROM SUCCESSFUL PROFESSIONALS

Resilience is not an abstract concept; it is a skill demonstrated by countless individuals who have turned setbacks into opportunities for reinvention. Consider the story of Oprah Winfrey, now one of the most influential media figures in history. Early in her career, Winfrey faced a significant professional rejection when she was fired from her job as a television news anchor in Baltimore. Her producers deemed her "unfit for television," citing her emotional involvement in stories as a flaw. Rather than accepting this as a definitive judgment on her capabilities, Winfrey pivoted. She embraced her ability to connect emotionally with audiences, a trait that became the cornerstone of *The Oprah Winfrey Show*. Her dismissal, rather than signaling the end of her career, set the stage for her rise as a cultural icon.

Another compelling example is J.K. Rowling, whose journey from obscurity to literary fame is a testament to perseverance. Before the publication of *Harry Potter and the Philosopher's Stone*, Rowling faced repeated rejections from major publishers. At one point, she was a struggling single mother, living on welfare and battling depression. Her manuscript was rejected by 12 publishers, many of whom doubted the market potential for a children's book about a young wizard.

Despite these setbacks, Rowling persisted, ultimately securing a deal with Bloomsbury Publishing. Today, her work has sold over 500 million copies worldwide, reshaping the landscape of modern literature. Rowling's story underscores how resilience, fueled by unwavering belief in one's vision, can transform adversity into unprecedented success.

Elon Musk, a figure synonymous with innovation, offers another example of resilience in the face of failure. Before Tesla became a dominant force in the electric vehicle industry, Musk encountered repeated challenges. Both Tesla and SpaceX teetered on the brink of bankruptcy, with SpaceX experiencing multiple high-profile rocket failures. In 2008, the company was down to its last launch attempt, and failure would have meant financial ruin. Against these odds, Musk invested his remaining resources, and SpaceX successfully launched its Falcon 1 rocket, securing critical contracts that kept the company afloat. Musk's ability to persist through financial strain and public skepticism highlights the power of resilience in overcoming seemingly insurmountable obstacles.

Even individuals in the creative arts, where rejection is particularly commonplace, exemplify resilience. Steven Spielberg, now one of the most celebrated directors in cinematic history, was famously rejected multiple times by the University of Southern California's School of Cinematic Arts. Rather than allowing these rejections to deter him, Spielberg pursued his passion independently, gaining hands-on experience that would later define his approach to filmmaking. His resilience paid off when his early work caught the attention of Hollywood, leading to a career that has redefined the industry.

These stories share a common thread: the ability to reframe failure not as an end, but as a detour. Oprah Winfrey channeled criticism into authenticity, J.K. Rowling turned rejection into resilience, Elon Musk transformed setbacks into strategy, and Steven Spielberg leveraged rejection as motivation. Their paths to success were neither linear nor easy, yet their resilience allowed them to transcend obstacles, proving that rejection, while painful, can become the foundation for extraordinary achievement. These examples serve as powerful reminders that setbacks are often the crucibles in which greatness is forged.

REFLECTION AND ACTION: REFRAMING FAILURE

Reframing failure begins with a shift in perspective. Instead of seeing it as an endpoint or an indictment of one's abilities, failure can be approached as a natural, even essential, part of growth. Reflection is the first step in this process. When confronted with rejection or setbacks, take time to assess the experience objectively. Ask questions such as: *What can I learn from this situation? What factors contributed to the outcome, and how might I approach things differently in the future?* These questions turn the focus away from self-criticism and toward constructive evaluation. Reflection transforms failure from a source of shame into an opportunity for self-awareness and improvement.

Another crucial step in reframing failure is identifying the underlying fears it often triggers. For many, failure taps into fears of inadequacy or rejection, which can lead to avoidance behaviors or paralyzing uncertainty. Recognizing these fears as natural but not insurmountable is vital. Acknowledge them without judgment, and take small, actionable steps to move forward. For instance, if fear of failure discourages someone from pursuing a promotion, breaking the process into manageable stages—such as acquiring specific skills or seeking mentorship—can help rebuild confidence. Reframing failure is not about eliminating fear but learning to coexist with it while taking proactive steps toward one's goals.

Taking deliberate action is the bridge between reframing failure and personal growth. Start by redefining success in broader, more personalized terms. Traditional definitions of success often revolve around external validation, such as promotions, accolades, or financial rewards. Instead, focus on metrics that align with intrinsic values, like learning new skills, building meaningful relationships, or pursuing a passion. This approach reduces the sting of individual failures by emphasizing long-term progress over immediate outcomes. For example, someone who didn't secure a job after an interview can view the experience as an opportunity to refine their interviewing skills, making them better prepared for future opportunities.

Practical tools can also aid in reframing failure. Journaling is one effective method, offering a space to process emotions and identify lessons from setbacks. Writing about a failure forces clarity, turning abstract feelings of disappointment into concrete observations and insights. Role-playing scenarios with trusted colleagues or mentors can provide another avenue for growth, simulating situations where past failures occurred and practicing improved responses. Such exercises not only build skills but also desensitize individuals to the fear of repeated failure, fostering a mindset of resilience.

By embracing reflection and purposeful action, failure loses its power to define or limit us. It becomes a stepping stone rather than a stumbling block—a momentary challenge that enriches personal and professional growth. This mindset, though not developed overnight, builds a stronger, more adaptable individual capable of navigating the inevitable ups and downs of a meaningful career. Failure, when reframed, transforms from an adversary into an ally, guiding us toward our greatest potential.

TURNING SETBACKS INTO STEPPING STONES

As we conclude this exploration of failure and resilience, it's essential to remember that setbacks are not just interruptions—they are invitations to grow, adapt, and redefine our paths. Each instance of rejection holds the potential to clarify what truly matters and to redirect us toward opportunities we might not have considered otherwise. When viewed through this lens, failure ceases to be an obstacle and becomes a powerful teacher, guiding us toward success with greater self-awareness and determination.

To transform setbacks into stepping stones, one must cultivate a habit of persistence. Resilience is not merely the ability to endure; it is the willingness to keep moving forward despite setbacks. History and personal experience alike reveal that breakthroughs often come after moments of profound disappointment. Think of an entrepreneur whose initial venture failed but whose lessons learned led to eventual triumph or an artist who found their voice only after years of rejection. These stories remind us that persistence is the bridge between failure and achievement, a quality accessible to all who choose to nurture it.

Equally important is embracing a mindset of curiosity and flexibility. Setbacks often signal areas where adaptation or a change in approach is necessary. By asking, *What else might work?* or *How can I pivot toward a better outcome?* individuals can uncover pathways they hadn't previously envisioned. This openness to experimentation not only mitigates the sting of failure but also expands possibilities for future growth. It is this capacity to pivot and innovate that distinguishes those who thrive in the face of challenges from those who are defeated by them.

Finally, celebrating small victories along the way reinforces the belief that growth is ongoing. After a setback, progress may seem slow or incremental, but even the smallest steps forward deserve acknowledgment. Recognizing these moments builds momentum, creating a sense of achievement that fuels further effort. Whether it's gaining new insight, completing a task outside one's comfort zone, or simply trying again after failure, these small wins collectively pave the way for larger successes.

Turning setbacks into stepping stones requires resilience, adaptability, and a commitment to learning. By adopting these principles, failure becomes less daunting and more empowering—a necessary stage in the pursuit of meaningful and lasting success. With this perspective, each rejection and setback serves not to hinder but to propel us forward, shaping not just our careers but our character and capacity to thrive.

Moving Forward

Setbacks often stir a whirlwind of emotions—frustration, sadness, anger, embarrassment, or even shame. These feelings, though uncomfortable, are a natural response to unmet expectations or perceived failure. Ignoring them doesn't diminish their intensity; instead, it often prolongs their impact. Recognizing and naming these emotions is a vital first step in the process of recovery. It is not a sign of weakness but an acknowledgment of the humanity behind ambition and effort. When people allow themselves to experience these emotions fully, they can better understand their root causes and move beyond them constructively.

Psychological research highlights the importance of emotional validation during difficult times. Studies show that suppressing negative feelings can lead to heightened stress levels, reduced cognitive clarity, and even physical symptoms like fatigue or tension. Acknowledging what you feel, whether disappointment in an opportunity lost or frustration at an obstacle, creates a foundation for emotional regulation. For example, a professional who admits their sadness over not landing a promotion may find it easier to focus on the practical next steps than someone who denies or represses that disappointment. This step fosters clarity and allows emotions to pass without overwhelming long-term decision-making.

Acknowledgment also invites self-compassion, a critical yet often overlooked aspect of resilience. It's common to harshly judge oneself after a setback, internalizing failure as personal inadequacy. However, such judgment compounds emotional distress and creates mental barriers to moving forward. Instead, adopting a more compassionate inner dialogue—recognizing that everyone encounters setbacks—can shift the narrative. Reflecting on past instances where challenges were overcome can remind individuals that failure is a shared experience, not a unique flaw. This shift in mindset is not about minimizing accountability but about cultivating the emotional balance necessary for growth.

Practical tools for emotional acknowledgment include journaling, mindfulness practices, and simply talking to a trusted friend or mentor. Writing down emotions can provide clarity and externalize what feels overwhelming. Mindfulness exercises, such as deep breathing or guided meditation, can help individuals remain present, creating space between their emotions and their reactions. Conversations with others often bring perspective, offering empathy and sometimes humor to alleviate emotional weight. By fully acknowledging and processing emotions, professionals create a mental environment conducive to proactive recovery and future success.

PROCESSING THE EXPERIENCE THROUGH REFLECTION

Reflection transforms setbacks from static disappointments into opportunities for insight and growth. Without reflection, failure risks becoming an unresolved weight that burdens future decisions. However, when individuals consciously process what happened and why, they often uncover valuable lessons that can inform their next steps. Reflection involves more than ruminating over what went wrong; it is a structured effort to understand the experience, draw conclusions, and identify pathways forward. This practice enables setbacks to act as stepping stones toward personal and professional development rather than obstacles to be avoided.

Effective reflection starts with asking the right questions. What factors contributed to the setback? Were they within your control, or were external circumstances at play? Did you underestimate challenges, overestimate resources, or fail to anticipate risks? These questions are not about assigning blame but about gaining clarity. For instance, a job candidate who didn't secure a role might reflect on their interview preparation, industry fit, or the employer's needs. By dissecting the experience, they might discover gaps in their skill set or areas where their strengths were not effectively communicated. Such insights can guide future efforts, transforming initial disappointment into actionable improvement.

Equally important is identifying the positive aspects of the experience. Even in failure, there are often elements of success—steps taken, risks embraced, or courage displayed. A professional who launched a business that later failed may reflect on their ability to execute a vision, build a network, or develop operational skills. Recognizing these achievements prevents a one-dimensional view of the setback and fosters self-confidence. It reframes the failure not as a complete loss but as a complex experience containing both challenges and victories. This balanced perspective nurtures resilience and ensures that future efforts are approached with both optimism and wisdom.

To deepen the reflective process, tools such as journaling, feedback sessions, or structured frameworks like SWOT analysis can be employed. Writing in a journal helps individuals articulate and organize their thoughts, revealing patterns or blind spots. Seeking feedback from colleagues or mentors adds an external perspective, often highlighting strengths or opportunities that self-assessment might miss. Using structured methods like SWOT (strengths, weaknesses, opportunities, threats) can transform abstract emotions into tangible insights. By reflecting deliberately and consistently, setbacks cease to be roadblocks and become valuable contributors to professional growth.

REGAINING CONFIDENCE WITH SMALL WINS

After experiencing a setback, confidence often takes a hit, making it difficult to approach future challenges with the same enthusiasm or assurance. Regaining that confidence starts with recalibrating expectations and focusing on achievable, incremental goals. Small wins—those modest yet meaningful accomplishments—act as building blocks for restoring self-belief. By concentrating on attainable tasks, individuals create a momentum that not only rebuilds their sense of competence but also reinforces their ability to navigate challenges effectively.

Psychologists often emphasize the importance of goal-setting theory in recovery from setbacks. Setting smaller, short-term goals creates a sense of purpose and agency. For example, someone recovering from a failed project at work might begin by tackling simpler, lower-stakes assignments to rebuild their confidence. Success in these smaller tasks restores trust in their abilities, laying the groundwork for tackling more significant challenges. These small victories also provide tangible evidence of progress, counteracting the self-doubt that often follows failure.

Another key advantage of small wins is their ability to reframe narratives around failure. Setbacks can create a cycle of negative self-talk, with individuals focusing on what they perceive as their inadequacies. Achieving smaller milestones interrupts this pattern, replacing it with positive reinforcement. Each win, no matter how minor, becomes a reminder of their capacity to succeed. A professional who struggles with public speaking, for example, might start by practicing in front of a small, supportive group rather than immediately diving into a high-pressure presentation. The success of this smaller effort builds the confidence needed to tackle larger audiences over time.

Practical strategies for pursuing small wins include breaking large goals into manageable tasks, celebrating progress, and enlisting support from mentors or peers. Breaking a daunting goal into smaller steps makes the process feel less overwhelming and allows for steady progress. Celebrating each achievement, no matter how minor, reinforces a sense of accomplishment. Engaging with mentors or colleagues adds accountability and encouragement, ensuring that efforts remain consistent. Through these small wins, individuals not only regain confidence but also rebuild the resilience needed to face future setbacks with courage and determination.

SEEKING CONSTRUCTIVE FEEDBACK

Constructive feedback is one of the most powerful tools for growth after a setback. It provides clarity, offering perspectives that individuals might overlook in the emotional aftermath of failure. Yet, seeking feedback requires vulnerability and courage, as it involves inviting critique during a period when confidence may already be fragile. However, when approached strategically, feedback becomes a catalyst for improvement, transforming uncertainty into actionable insight and preparing individuals to approach future challenges with renewed strength.

The first step in seeking feedback is identifying the right sources. Not all critiques are created equal; feedback should come from individuals who understand your goals, have expertise in the relevant area, and genuinely want to support your growth. For instance, a professional who struggled during a team project might turn to a trusted colleague, a manager, or even an external mentor for perspective. Feedback from these sources tends to be balanced and actionable, focusing on improvement rather than assigning blame. Seeking out those who offer honesty and encouragement in equal measure is essential to making feedback a constructive experience.

When soliciting feedback, specificity matters. Open-ended requests like "What do you think I did wrong?" often yield vague or overly critical responses. Instead, framing questions around particular aspects of the experience invites focused and helpful input. For example, asking "How could I improve my communication during meetings?" or "Were there specific areas where my analysis fell short?" encourages responses that highlight clear opportunities for growth. Structured inquiries not only guide the feedback provider but also help the recipient avoid becoming overwhelmed by unrelated or unhelpful commentary.

Finally, the way feedback is received determines its impact. Defensive reactions or an unwillingness to consider alternative viewpoints can undermine the value of even the most insightful critique. Approaching feedback with a mindset of curiosity and openness ensures that lessons are absorbed rather than dismissed. Taking notes, asking follow-up questions, and expressing gratitude to the feedback provider all signal a commitment to growth. Over time, this practice fosters a culture of self-improvement, where setbacks become opportunities to refine skills, gain clarity, and build resilience. Feedback, when embraced fully, is not a reminder of failure but a roadmap to future success.

BUILDING A SUPPORTIVE NETWORK

Recovering from setbacks is rarely a solo endeavor; the presence of a supportive network can make the difference between feeling isolated in failure and finding the strength to move forward. A well-connected community provides encouragement, guidance, and the reassurance that setbacks are a shared human experience, not a personal flaw. This network acts as a buffer against the emotional toll of failure, offering both practical advice and emotional support to help individuals navigate difficult moments.

A supportive network begins with diversity. Surrounding yourself with people who bring different perspectives enriches the recovery process. For instance, mentors can provide wisdom gained from their own experiences, while peers might offer relatable stories of setbacks and successes. Colleagues and friends often serve as sounding boards, helping to process emotions or brainstorm solutions. Even professional networks, such as industry groups or online forums, can offer invaluable insights and connections that help redirect focus from failure to opportunity. Each layer of this network contributes a unique form of support, creating a well-rounded foundation for resilience.

One of the key benefits of a strong network is the normalization of setbacks. When individuals share their experiences, it becomes clear that failure is not an anomaly but a natural part of growth. This shared understanding reduces the stigma of failure and fosters a sense of belonging. For example, hearing a mentor recount how they bounced back after being passed over for a promotion can inspire others to view their own rejections with greater perspective. The realization that even successful professionals have encountered obstacles reinforces the idea that failure is not the end of the journey but a stepping stone toward eventual success.

Building and maintaining a supportive network requires intentional effort. Nurturing relationships involves showing up for others, being willing to listen, and offering help when needed. It also means seeking out new connections, whether by attending professional events, joining interest-based communities, or reaching out to individuals whose experiences align with your own challenges. Importantly, this effort should be reciprocal; as much as you draw from the network, contributing to it ensures that it remains vibrant and mutually beneficial. Over time, a well-built network becomes not just a source of resilience but a critical element in personal and professional growth.

SHIFTING FOCUS TO LONG-TERM GROWTH

One of the most transformative ways to recover from setbacks is to reframe them as steps in a larger journey rather than isolated failures. Shifting focus to long-term growth allows individuals to view challenges through a broader lens, where every experience—whether success or setback—becomes part of their personal and professional evolution. This perspective fosters patience, resilience, and a forward-thinking mindset that emphasizes continuous improvement over immediate results.

The first step in embracing long-term growth is redefining success. Traditional definitions often emphasize short-term achievements, such as hitting specific targets or securing promotions, which can amplify the sting of failure when these goals are unmet. Instead, individuals can benefit from adopting a growth-oriented definition of success that values learning, skill-building, and adaptability. For instance, someone who lost a major client might focus not only on the loss but also on the negotiation skills they developed or the lessons learned about client retention. This reframing transforms the experience into an asset for future endeavors.

Cultivating a growth mindset also involves setting goals that prioritize progress over perfection. Long-term growth is not about avoiding setbacks but using them to inform and refine future strategies. For example, rather than dwelling on a poorly received presentation, an individual could set a goal to improve their public speaking skills over the next six months by joining a speaking group or taking a course. These incremental, achievable objectives help maintain momentum, even after failures, and provide tangible evidence of growth over time.

Another critical element of focusing on long-term growth is patience. In a culture that often celebrates instant gratification, setbacks can feel like roadblocks to success. However, most meaningful achievements require sustained effort and perseverance. Consider the careers of renowned professionals or entrepreneurs who often faced repeated failures before achieving lasting success. Their stories highlight the importance of viewing setbacks not as endpoints but as temporary detours on the path to growth. Emulating this mindset encourages individuals to stay committed to their long-term vision, even when immediate results are disappointing.

By shifting focus from short-term disappointments to the broader narrative of personal development, individuals can transform how they respond to challenges. This long-term perspective not only softens the impact of failure but also builds resilience, ensuring that each setback becomes an integral part of their journey toward greater achievements and fulfillment. Over time, this approach fosters a profound sense of purpose, reminding individuals that growth is a lifelong process and that setbacks are merely chapters in a much larger story of success.

DEVELOPING A RESILIENCE TOOLKIT

Building resilience after setbacks requires more than a single strategy; it involves cultivating a set of tools and practices that can be drawn upon in moments of adversity. A resilience toolkit is a personalized collection of methods, habits, and resources designed to help individuals navigate challenges, process emotions, and emerge stronger. By proactively developing this toolkit, people can prepare themselves to face future setbacks with confidence and adaptability.

The foundation of a resilience toolkit lies in self-awareness. Understanding your triggers, emotional responses, and coping mechanisms allows you to identify which tools are most effective in different situations. For instance, journaling might help some individuals gain clarity after a professional rejection, while others may find solace in talking through their experience with a trusted mentor. Regular self-assessment exercises, such as reflecting on past challenges and how they were managed, can reveal patterns and highlight areas for growth. This awareness ensures that the toolkit remains dynamic and responsive to individual needs.

Practical tools form the core of the resilience toolkit. These might include mindfulness practices, such as meditation or deep-breathing exercises, to calm the mind during moments of stress. Physical activities like yoga or jogging can help release tension and foster a sense of control over the body and mind. Professional resources, such as books, courses, or career coaching, provide actionable insights and strategies to rebuild confidence and regain focus. The inclusion of diverse tools ensures that individuals have multiple avenues for recovery, catering to both emotional well-being and professional growth.

Building a resilience toolkit also involves creating systems of support. This includes identifying people within your network who can offer advice, encouragement, or a listening ear when setbacks occur. For example, maintaining a regular check-in with a mentor or peer group creates a safe space to share challenges and gain perspective. Digital tools, such as productivity apps or habit trackers, can also play a role by helping to establish routines that support resilience, such as setting small, achievable goals or celebrating milestones of progress.

Finally, a resilience toolkit must evolve with time and experience. As individuals grow and encounter new challenges, they may find that certain tools lose relevance while others become indispensable. Periodic evaluation of the toolkit ensures that it remains effective and aligned with current needs. By developing and refining this toolkit, individuals create a reliable framework for navigating setbacks, ensuring that they can bounce back with clarity, strength, and a renewed sense of purpose.

CLOSING ENCOURAGEMENT

Resilience is not an innate trait possessed by the fortunate few; it is a skill cultivated through intention, effort, and persistence. The path to bouncing back from setbacks is not always linear, but it is always within reach. Setbacks, though painful in the moment, are not indicators of failure but opportunities for transformation. They provide the space to reassess priorities, rediscover inner strength, and redefine the journey forward.

As you reflect on the tools and strategies outlined in this chapter, remember that resilience is built one choice at a time. Each time you process a disappointment, reach out for support, or take a small step toward a new goal, you are strengthening your ability to weather future challenges. These moments of growth, though subtle, accumulate over time to form a foundation of confidence and fortitude. Trust in this process and in your capacity to rise stronger after each fall.

It is also important to remember that setbacks are universal. Even the most successful individuals have faced rejection, criticism, and failure. Their stories reveal that resilience is not about avoiding difficulty but about confronting it with courage and adaptability. Let their experiences remind you that you, too, are capable of overcoming obstacles and continuing toward your goals, no matter how daunting they may seem in the present.

In moving forward, embrace setbacks as integral to your story rather than deviations from it. Each challenge faced and overcome adds depth to your character, making the successes ahead even more meaningful. Resilience is not about perfection; it is about progress. With the right mindset, tools, and support, you can turn every setback into a stepping stone toward a future of growth and fulfillment. Keep moving forward with determination and faith in your ability to thrive.

Chapter 7: Cultivating a Growth Mindset

Our perspective shapes the way we approach and interpret the challenges we face. For many, challenges in the workplace—whether it's a missed promotion, a difficult project, or navigating office dynamics—can feel like threats to their competence or value. This response is rooted in the natural fear of failure or rejection, which triggers insecurity and often leads to avoidance or self-doubt. However, by shifting our perspective, we can transform these moments into opportunities for growth and self-improvement. This section sets the stage for understanding how a shift in mindset can lead to both personal and professional empowerment.

The concept of viewing challenges as opportunities is deeply tied to the idea of a growth mindset, a term popularized by psychologist Carol Dweck. A growth mindset involves believing that abilities and intelligence can be developed through effort, learning, and persistence. In contrast, a fixed mindset sees abilities as static and unchangeable. When challenges arise, those with a fixed mindset may see them as insurmountable barriers, whereas those with a growth mindset recognize them as stepping stones for development. By cultivating this perspective, we can begin to see obstacles not as reflections of inadequacy, but as moments of valuable learning.

Insecurity often distorts our ability to adopt a growth-oriented perspective. When faced with challenges, it's common to fixate on worst-case scenarios or interpret setbacks as proof of personal failure. For example, receiving critical feedback from a manager might initially feel like a personal attack, reinforcing fears of not being good enough. Yet, this same feedback could be viewed as constructive guidance—a chance to refine skills or address blind spots. The key lies in the way we interpret the situation, which can either deepen insecurity or foster resilience and growth.

A shift in perspective doesn't mean ignoring or minimizing difficulties. It's about reframing them in a way that aligns with long-term goals and personal development. A challenge is often a signpost pointing toward an area that requires attention, effort, and growth. By choosing to see these moments as opportunities rather than obstacles, we open ourselves to new possibilities, whether it's learning a new skill, developing patience, or building stronger relationships. This change begins with acknowledging that how we perceive a challenge is just as important as the challenge itself.

THE PSYCHOLOGICAL BASIS OF REFRAMING

Reframing challenges as opportunities is not just a feel-good philosophy; it is deeply rooted in psychological principles that influence how we process experiences. Central to this is the concept of neuroplasticity, which refers to the brain's ability to reorganize itself by forming new neural connections throughout life. Each time we face a challenge and approach it with a mindset of learning, the brain adapts, creating pathways that strengthen our ability to solve problems and manage similar situations in the future. In contrast, avoidance or negative self-talk can reinforce neural patterns associated with fear and insecurity, making it harder to approach challenges with confidence.

Cognitive reframing, a core technique in cognitive-behavioral therapy (CBT), demonstrates the power of shifting one's mindset. This process involves identifying negative or unhelpful thoughts and reinterpreting them in a more constructive way. For example, instead of thinking, "I'm terrible at this task, and everyone will notice," you might reframe it as, "This task is new to me, but I can use this as a chance to improve." By consciously altering the narrative, you change your emotional response to the challenge, reducing anxiety and fostering a sense of agency. This principle can be applied broadly to workplace scenarios, from navigating complex projects to handling difficult conversations with colleagues.

Research also highlights how our interpretation of stress impacts its effect on our well-being. Studies have shown that viewing stress as a challenge rather than a threat can lead to better performance and health outcomes. For example, a study by the American Psychological Association found that participants who were encouraged to reinterpret stress as an energizing force performed better on tasks and reported lower levels of anxiety. This "stress-is-enhancing" mindset aligns closely with the practice of reframing challenges, emphasizing that our perception can dictate not only how we feel but also how we perform.

Finally, reframing is tied to the principle of self-efficacy—the belief in our ability to influence outcomes. Challenges often feel overwhelming because they seem beyond our control, feeding into a cycle of insecurity and passivity. However, when we reframe these situations as opportunities to exercise and grow our capabilities, we reinforce our sense of self-efficacy. This shift empowers us to take actionable steps, even in the face of adversity, creating a positive feedback loop that builds confidence and resilience over time. By understanding these psychological foundations, we can appreciate the transformative power of reframing and start applying it in our professional lives.

RELATABLE ANECDOTES OR CASE STUDIES

Stories of others navigating challenges provide powerful examples of how reframing can transform adversity into opportunity. These real-life anecdotes illustrate how individuals from diverse backgrounds and industries have shifted their perspectives to overcome insecurity and achieve growth. Such stories not only inspire but also make the concept of reframing more tangible and relatable for readers.

One illustrative case is that of Priya, a new graduate who landed her first job in a competitive corporate environment. Initially, Priya felt overwhelmed by her responsibilities and the steep learning curve. Her insecurity amplified every time she made a mistake, convincing her she was out of her depth. However, with the guidance of a mentor, Priya began to view her errors as learning opportunities rather than failures. She started keeping a journal to reflect on her mistakes and document what she had learned from them. Over time, this practice allowed her to see progress and reduced her fear of taking on challenging tasks. By reframing her perspective, Priya not only became more competent in her role but also gained the confidence to take on larger responsibilities, eventually earning a promotion within two years.

Another example involves James, a mid-career professional who faced a significant setback when a project he led failed to meet expectations. Initially, James was consumed by self-doubt, interpreting the failure as a sign he was not leadership material. However, after a candid discussion with his supervisor, he realized the project had faltered due to a lack of communication within the team, not because of his leadership abilities. By reframing the experience as a valuable lesson in team dynamics, James worked to improve his communication skills and implemented regular feedback sessions with his team. Within a year, James successfully led a high-profile project, turning his initial setback into a stepping stone for professional growth.

On a broader scale, the story of a small business owner adapting to economic challenges offers a powerful example of reframing. Maria, the owner of a boutique retail shop, saw her business hit hard by the pandemic, with foot traffic dropping dramatically. While the initial shock left her questioning her future,

Maria decided to view the situation as an opportunity to pivot. She quickly built an e-commerce platform, expanded her social media presence, and offered virtual shopping experiences. By shifting her perspective, Maria not only kept her business afloat but also reached a larger customer base than she had pre-pandemic.

These stories underscore a common theme: challenges can be reframed into opportunities for growth, learning, and innovation. Whether it's a young professional, an experienced leader, or an entrepreneur, the act of changing how one perceives a setback can make all the difference. For readers, these anecdotes offer both inspiration and practical proof that adopting a growth mindset can lead to significant professional and personal transformation.

PRACTICAL STEPS TO SHIFT PERSPECTIVES

Shifting perspectives from viewing challenges as threats to seeing them as opportunities is not an innate skill but a practice that requires deliberate effort. By adopting specific strategies, individuals can train their minds to reframe challenges constructively. These steps offer actionable techniques to help readers develop this mindset in their daily professional lives.

The first step is to recognize and challenge automatic negative thoughts. When faced with a challenge, the brain often defaults to a negative narrative driven by insecurity. Thoughts like "I'm not good enough" or "This will ruin my career" can dominate, making the situation feel insurmountable. To counter this, it's essential to pause and identify these automatic responses. Write them down, then question their validity: Is this thought based on facts or assumptions? Reframing involves replacing these thoughts with constructive alternatives. For instance, instead of "I failed at this task," try "This didn't work out as planned, but now I know what to improve." This small shift can significantly impact emotional and behavioral responses to challenges.

Another practical approach is to adopt a learner's mindset by viewing challenges as experiments rather than tests of competence. This perspective encourages curiosity and reduces the fear of failure. For example, if a presentation at work doesn't go as expected, focus on what went well and what can be improved for next time, rather than dwelling on perceived inadequacies. Asking questions like "What can I learn from this?" or "How can I approach this differently next time?" can transform a setback into a stepping stone for growth. Keeping a "learning log" to document these insights further reinforces this mindset over time.

A third strategy is to shift focus from outcomes to effort and progress. Insecurity often stems from tying self-worth to external achievements, such as promotions or accolades. Reframing involves valuing the effort invested and the skills gained, regardless of the result. Celebrate small wins, like mastering a new tool or improving communication skills during a challenging project. This focus on progress builds resilience and motivates individuals to embrace challenges as opportunities for self-improvement, rather than as threats to their identity.

Finally, practice perspective-switching exercises to reframe challenges in real-time. One effective method is to imagine how a trusted mentor or colleague might view the same situation. What advice would they give? Alternatively, step back and view the challenge from a long-term perspective: Will this issue matter a year from now? These exercises help to distance oneself from immediate emotional reactions, making it easier to see the bigger picture. By practicing this regularly, reframing becomes a natural and automatic response.

These steps are not about denying the difficulties of challenges but about reframing them in ways that empower rather than paralyze. By recognizing negative thought patterns, focusing on learning, valuing progress, and using perspective-switching techniques, individuals can cultivate a growth-oriented mindset that turns professional obstacles into powerful opportunities for advancement.

BENEFITS OF EMBRACING CHALLENGES

Embracing challenges is not merely about enduring difficulties—it's about leveraging them to unlock personal and professional growth. When individuals shift their mindset to view challenges as opportunities, they open the door to numerous benefits that can transform their approach to work, relationships, and self-perception. These benefits extend beyond immediate problem-solving, creating long-term advantages in confidence, resilience, and achievement.

One of the most immediate benefits is enhanced learning and skill development. Challenges often push individuals outside their comfort zones, forcing them to acquire new skills, adapt to unfamiliar circumstances, or approach problems creatively. For instance, taking on a high-stakes project at work might require developing expertise in an unfamiliar area or collaborating with diverse teams. While daunting at first, these experiences broaden skillsets and prepare individuals for future responsibilities. By embracing such opportunities, professionals accelerate their growth, often gaining capabilities that distinguish them from their peers.

Another significant advantage is the building of resilience and mental toughness. Each time a challenge is met with persistence and effort, individuals strengthen their ability to cope with adversity. Resilience is like a muscle—it grows stronger with use. Facing and overcoming workplace difficulties, such as navigating a tough negotiation or recovering from a failed pitch, teaches individuals how to manage stress and bounce back from setbacks. Over time, these experiences foster a mindset that is not easily deterred by obstacles, creating a solid foundation for handling even greater challenges with composure and determination.

Embracing challenges also leads to greater confidence and self-efficacy. Every challenge successfully tackled reinforces the belief that one is capable of influencing outcomes. This growing confidence translates into a willingness to take on more significant responsibilities, pursue ambitious goals, and advocate for oneself in the workplace. For example, an employee who successfully leads a difficult project may feel more empowered to negotiate a promotion or present innovative ideas to leadership. This sense of agency not only benefits the individual but also makes them a more valuable contributor to their organization.

Finally, embracing challenges fosters a deeper sense of purpose and fulfillment. Challenges often align with personal or professional aspirations, whether it's mastering a complex skill, advancing in a career, or making a meaningful impact in a role. Confronting and overcoming obstacles in pursuit of these goals can lead to immense satisfaction and a stronger connection to one's work. Furthermore, the act of persevering through difficulties instills pride and a sense of accomplishment that can be profoundly motivating. Over time, individuals who embrace challenges are more likely to find their work meaningful and rewarding, driving sustained engagement and success.

In sum, embracing challenges is a transformative practice that builds skills, strengthens resilience, boosts confidence, and enhances fulfillment. While the initial steps may feel daunting, the rewards far outweigh the discomfort of stepping into the unknown. By shifting their perspective to see challenges as opportunities, individuals unlock their potential and position themselves for sustained personal and professional growth.

ACTIONABLE TAKEAWAYS

To make the shift in perspective from viewing challenges as threats to embracing them as opportunities for growth, it is essential to develop actionable habits that not only support this mindset but also make it sustainable over time. Below, we'll delve deeper into the practices that can reinforce this reframing process, ensuring that readers are equipped to tackle challenges with a growth-oriented approach.

Start a Reflection Practice

Reflection is a cornerstone of shifting perspectives, as it helps individuals examine their experiences from a different angle. To fully embrace this practice, it's crucial to make it a consistent, intentional habit. Begin by setting aside 10-15 minutes at the end of each workday or week to reflect on the challenges faced. This isn't just about recounting difficulties; it's about analyzing the lessons within those experiences.

For example, after a difficult presentation, ask yourself: "What worked well during this presentation? What could I improve for next time? How did I handle the nerves, and what can I learn from that?" These questions help you process the situation as a learning experience rather than a failure. Journaling these thoughts creates a valuable resource for revisiting and refining your approach in the future. Over time, this practice trains the brain to default to a growth-focused mindset when challenges arise, as reflection becomes synonymous with learning and progress. Additionally, revisiting past reflections will reveal patterns in how you have successfully navigated challenges, reinforcing the understanding that growth is a continuous journey.

Reframe Negative Thoughts in Real-Time

In the midst of a challenge, our minds often flood with negative thoughts. These automatic thoughts, such as "I'm not good enough" or "I'll never succeed," can hinder our ability to take action or find solutions. To counteract these, practice **real-time cognitive reframing**. When these thoughts emerge, pause and notice them. Acknowledge the emotion behind them without judgment—

whether it's fear, doubt, or frustration—and then consciously replace these thoughts with more constructive and empowering ones.

For instance, if you're struggling with a complex task, the thought "I'm terrible at this" might arise. Instead of letting that thought dictate your behavior, reframe it by thinking, "This task is tough, but I can break it down into smaller, manageable pieces. Each step I take brings me closer to understanding it." By training yourself to pause and reframe in real-time, you shift the focus from limitations to possibilities. Over time, this becomes an automatic response, making it easier to confront challenges with a positive and productive mindset.

Celebrate Effort and Small Wins

The tendency to focus only on outcomes—such as project success, promotions, or accolades—can create unnecessary pressure and reinforce the idea that anything less than perfection is a failure. To counteract this, it is essential to shift the focus to effort and progress. Recognize the hard work, persistence, and bravery it took to face the challenge in the first place. Even if the final result didn't meet expectations, the effort itself is valuable and worthy of celebration.

Small wins, such as improving a skill, learning something new, or navigating a difficult situation with poise, should be celebrated just as much as major successes. For example, after presenting an idea at a meeting, acknowledge the courage it took to speak up, the clarity you gained through preparing, and the feedback you received—regardless of whether your idea was accepted. Create personal rewards for these milestones, such as a relaxing break, a treat, or time spent on something you enjoy. This rewards system not only reinforces the effort but also builds self-esteem. Over time, you'll find that celebrating small wins keeps you motivated, reduces the pressure to achieve perfect outcomes, and fosters a sense of accomplishment with each challenge faced.

Use Visualization to Shift Mindset

Visualization is a powerful cognitive tool used by athletes, performers, and high achievers to prepare for success. It involves mentally rehearsing a task or goal and imagining yourself succeeding. This technique works because the brain doesn't always differentiate between vividly imagined experiences and actual ones, so by mentally rehearsing success, you prime your mind and body to perform at their best.

To use visualization effectively, take a few moments before encountering a challenge—whether it's a difficult conversation with a manager, a presentation, or a new project—and vividly imagine yourself handling it with confidence and poise. Picture yourself managing obstacles smoothly and achieving the desired outcome. Focus on how you'll feel after the challenge is overcome: empowered, accomplished, and proud. The more you visualize success in the context of challenges, the more you will build confidence in your ability to handle them. This mental preparation helps reduce anxiety and increases the likelihood of a positive outcome.

Visualization can be especially helpful when facing recurring challenges or tasks that provoke anxiety. For example, if you have an upcoming performance review, visualize not only the conversation but also the positive actions you'll take to address feedback. Imagine how you will speak about your accomplishments, and mentally rehearse handling any critical comments constructively. By seeing yourself succeed in your mind first, you reduce the mental roadblocks that often hold you back in reality.

Seek Support and Feedback

Embracing challenges is made easier when you have a supportive network to help you gain perspective and feedback. While reframing can be an internal process, external validation and advice can offer invaluable insights. This could involve seeking support from a mentor, colleague, or even a friend outside of the workplace. When you encounter a difficult challenge, discuss it with someone who can offer a different perspective or advice. This often helps you see the situation from a more objective, constructive angle.

In addition to support, actively seek feedback after confronting a challenge, whether the outcome was positive or negative. Feedback is essential not only for growth but also for reaffirming your ability to improve. Whether it's feedback from your manager after a project or constructive criticism from a peer, view these conversations as opportunities to learn and fine-tune your approach. Ask questions like, "What went well in this project? What can I improve for next time?" Feedback helps you refine your skills, identify blind spots, and build a more effective strategy for handling future challenges.

Over time, regular feedback and support will reinforce the notion that challenges are not obstacles to be feared, but rather opportunities to learn and evolve. A strong support system also provides encouragement and reassurance, helping you build the confidence to tackle increasingly difficult challenges.

By incorporating these in-depth strategies into your daily routine, you'll begin to naturally shift your perspective toward seeing challenges as opportunities for growth. This shift is a gradual process, but with consistent practice, you will foster a mindset that welcomes challenges, builds resilience, and leads to long-term success.

Daily Practices

The way we perceive the world shapes our experiences within it. Challenges, setbacks, and even mundane tasks can either feel overwhelming or empowering, depending on how we frame them. This is why perspective matters—it is the lens through which we interpret and react to the events of our lives. While circumstances themselves may remain constant, the ability to shift our perspective transforms those circumstances from obstacles into opportunities for growth.

For example, encountering failure can lead to self-doubt and avoidance of future risks, or it can serve as a powerful teacher, guiding us toward improvement. The key difference lies in how we view the situation. A fixed perspective sees failure as a personal deficiency, while a growth-oriented perspective recognizes it as a natural and necessary part of the learning process. This subtle shift in viewpoint does not erase the difficulty of the experience but reframes its significance in a way that fosters resilience and learning.

Perspective is not just an abstract concept; it has tangible effects on our emotions, behaviors, and outcomes. Neuroscience tells us that the brain is remarkably adaptable, capable of reshaping itself based on repeated thought patterns. When we consciously practice viewing challenges as opportunities, we train our minds to focus on potential solutions rather than problems. This reduces stress, enhances creativity, and equips us to respond to adversity more effectively. It's a practice that requires intention, but over time, it becomes a natural part of how we think.

Daily practices for mindfulness, gratitude, and confidence are among the most effective ways to cultivate a growth-oriented perspective. These habits provide tools for staying present, appreciating progress, and recognizing personal strength, even in the face of difficulty. By integrating these practices into daily life, we begin to reshape our mental frameworks, ensuring that we meet challenges with clarity, optimism, and self-assurance. This chapter explores how these exercises work, why they matter, and how they can create lasting change in the way we view ourselves and the world.

EXERCISES FOR MINDFULNESS

Mindfulness is the foundation for emotional resilience and mental clarity. It is the practice of anchoring oneself in the present moment, fully aware of thoughts, feelings, and surroundings without judgment. While this may sound simple, its effects on the mind and body are profound. In a world that often demands constant multitasking and productivity, mindfulness serves as a counterbalance, allowing individuals to pause, reflect, and respond thoughtfully rather than react impulsively.

One of the simplest yet most effective mindfulness practices is mindful breathing. This involves focusing solely on the breath, observing each inhale and exhale as they occur. This exercise, which can take as little as three to five minutes, helps to calm the nervous system, reduce stress, and improve concentration. For example, a professional preparing for a high-stakes meeting might use mindful breathing to steady their nerves and approach the situation with greater composure. Over time, this practice strengthens the ability to remain centered, even in high-pressure scenarios.

Another powerful technique is the body scan meditation. This involves systematically bringing attention to different parts of the body, noting any tension, discomfort, or sensation without judgment. By doing this, individuals develop a deeper connection to their physical state and learn to release tension they might not have even realized they were holding. This practice is particularly beneficial for those in physically demanding or high-stress professions, as it promotes relaxation and awareness of how the body responds to stress.

Mindful journaling is another valuable tool for cultivating awareness. Unlike traditional journaling, which often focuses on events or emotions, mindful journaling encourages individuals to observe and record their thoughts in the moment without analyzing or judging them. For example, writing about an emotionally charged situation with mindfulness might involve simply noting, "I feel frustration rising as I think about today's meeting," rather than trying to justify or suppress the feeling. This process creates a safe space for self-reflection, helping individuals to identify patterns in their thinking and better understand their emotional triggers.

Through these exercises, mindfulness becomes more than a temporary state; it becomes a skill that permeates daily life. Whether used to manage a difficult conversation, navigate a demanding workload, or simply find moments of peace in a busy day, mindfulness equips individuals to approach life with greater clarity and intention. As readers incorporate these practices into their routines, they will begin to notice subtle yet meaningful changes in their emotional well-being, decision-making, and overall sense of control.

CULTIVATING GRATITUDE

Gratitude is a powerful yet often underestimated practice that can transform the way we perceive our lives. By intentionally focusing on the positive aspects of our experiences, we rewire our brains to notice abundance instead of scarcity, opportunities instead of setbacks. Cultivating gratitude doesn't mean ignoring challenges or pretending problems don't exist; rather, it is about acknowledging the good alongside the difficult and recognizing the value of even the smallest blessings. This mindset shifts our focus from what we lack to what we have, creating a foundation for resilience and optimism.

Research shows that gratitude has tangible psychological and physiological benefits. Studies in positive psychology reveal that individuals who regularly practice gratitude report higher levels of happiness, reduced stress, and improved relationships. Neuroscience further supports this by demonstrating how gratitude activates the brain's reward centers, releasing feel-good chemicals like dopamine and serotonin. Over time, these repeated activations help create neural pathways that predispose us to seek and recognize positivity. Essentially, practicing gratitude is like training the mind to find light even in the darkest situations.

A simple yet impactful way to cultivate gratitude is through journaling. Setting aside just five minutes a day to list three things you are grateful for can create profound changes in mindset. These don't need to be grandiose moments; they can be as simple as a kind word from a colleague, a meal that brought comfort, or the feeling of sunshine on your face. Over time, this practice trains the mind to automatically scan for positives throughout the day, fostering a habit of appreciation that extends far beyond the pages of the journal.

Expressing gratitude to others is another transformative exercise. Taking the time to thank a coworker for their support or acknowledging a friend's thoughtfulness strengthens connections and fosters goodwill. For example, sending a quick email to a team member to highlight their contributions on a project not only boosts their morale but also enhances your own sense of connection and fulfillment. Gratitude, in this way, becomes a tool not just for personal growth but for building a more harmonious and supportive environment.

By incorporating gratitude into daily life, we create a buffer against negativity and a wellspring of positivity to draw from during challenging times. This practice doesn't eliminate difficulties but equips us with the perspective and strength to face them with grace. As readers begin to embrace gratitude, they will likely notice a ripple effect—improved mood, stronger relationships, and a greater sense of satisfaction with their personal and professional lives. Over time, gratitude becomes not just an exercise but a way of being, one that enriches every aspect of life.

BUILDING SELF-CONFIDENCE OVER TIME

Self-confidence is not an innate trait reserved for a lucky few—it is a skill that anyone can develop with time and deliberate effort. Building self-confidence involves cultivating a belief in one's abilities and worth, independent of external validation. It requires consistent, intentional actions that shift self-perception from doubt to assurance. While the process may take time, each small step creates momentum, eventually transforming self-doubt into self-trust.

One of the most effective ways to build confidence is through incremental risk-taking. These "micro-risks" involve stepping slightly out of one's comfort zone in manageable ways. For example, speaking up during a team meeting or volunteering for a small project might feel daunting at first, but each success reinforces the belief that one is capable. Over time, these small acts accumulate, creating a foundation of confidence that can support larger challenges. The key is to start small and build gradually, ensuring each step feels achievable while still promoting growth.

Another cornerstone of confidence-building is positive self-talk. Many people unconsciously sabotage their self-esteem with negative inner dialogues—statements like "I'm not good enough" or "I always mess up." Replacing these thoughts with affirming statements, such as "I am capable" or "I am learning and improving," can have a profound impact. While this might feel forced initially, repetition helps these affirmations take root, gradually reshaping the internal narrative. Writing these affirmations in a journal or reciting them during moments of doubt can amplify their effect, reinforcing a more empowering self-image.

Tracking and celebrating personal achievements is another critical practice. A "success journal" can be a powerful tool for this purpose, allowing individuals to record daily accomplishments, no matter how small. These might include completing a challenging task, navigating a difficult conversation, or even simply showing resilience in the face of adversity. By reflecting on these wins, individuals build evidence of their competence and resilience, which counters feelings of inadequacy. This practice also shifts focus away from failures or shortcomings, emphasizing growth and progress instead.

Building self-confidence is not about eliminating fear or doubt but about learning to act despite them. It is about creating a solid sense of self that remains steady in the face of criticism, rejection, or setbacks. This process requires patience, as genuine confidence develops over time through consistent practice and reflection. However, as readers commit to these practices, they will begin to notice subtle but significant changes—not only in how they perceive themselves but also in how they navigate the world. Confidence becomes less about proving oneself to others and more about trusting one's own ability to rise to any occasion.

INTEGRATION INTO DAILY LIFE

While mindfulness, gratitude, and self-confidence practices are transformative, their true power lies in consistent application. Integrating these habits into daily life ensures they become second nature, shaping thoughts, behaviors, and reactions over time. This process of integration doesn't require a complete overhaul of one's routine. Instead, it involves weaving small, intentional actions into the fabric of everyday life, gradually creating a lifestyle rooted in awareness, appreciation, and self-assurance.

Start by identifying natural opportunities within your day for these practices. For mindfulness, moments like a morning coffee break or a commute can be repurposed into intentional pauses. Instead of scrolling through emails or social media, focus on the warmth of the cup in your hands, the aroma of the coffee, or the sensation of your breath as it flows in and out. These micro-moments of mindfulness build presence without adding extra tasks to your day. Over time, they serve as anchors, helping you return to calm and clarity amidst the chaos of daily responsibilities.

Gratitude can be seamlessly integrated through brief reflections during transitions, such as before meals or bedtime. Consider pairing gratitude with an existing habit—like brushing your teeth or setting an alarm—to reinforce consistency. For example, as you wind down for the night, think of three things that went well during the day. Writing these in a journal or simply saying them aloud shifts your focus from what's missing to what's present, reinforcing a positive outlook before sleep. With practice, this simple act becomes a natural part of your routine, fostering a grateful mindset that endures throughout the day.

Building self-confidence also benefits from consistent daily actions. Set aside a few minutes each day to acknowledge one thing you did well, no matter how small. This could be something as simple as completing a task you were dreading or navigating a tough conversation with composure. Pair this reflection with a forward-looking affirmation, such as "Tomorrow, I will approach challenges with curiosity and strength." These daily moments of acknowledgment and intention serve as powerful reminders of your growth and capability, reinforcing confidence incrementally.

The key to successful integration is simplicity and sustainability. Overloading your routine with ambitious practices can lead to burnout, undermining the very goals you're trying to achieve. Instead, focus on small, manageable changes that align with your current habits and schedule. As these practices become habitual, they require less conscious effort, eventually blending seamlessly into your life. Integration, then, is not about perfection but persistence—choosing to show up for yourself in small but meaningful ways each day. This steady commitment transforms mindfulness, gratitude, and self-confidence from abstract ideals into tangible, lived experiences.

BENEFITS OF SUSTAINED PRACTICE

The cumulative benefits of sustained practice in mindfulness, gratitude, and self-confidence extend far beyond the immediate effects of each exercise. When these practices become a regular part of daily life, they begin to fundamentally reshape one's outlook, resilience, and overall well-being. The consistent, small actions taken each day build upon one another, fostering a mental and emotional landscape where positivity, focus, and self-assurance become the norm rather than the exception. These changes are gradual but profound, creating a solid foundation for navigating life's inevitable ups and downs with greater grace and strength.

One of the primary benefits of sustained practice is increased emotional resilience. Daily mindfulness strengthens the ability to stay calm and composed, even in high-stress situations, by training the mind to focus on the present moment rather than getting lost in anxious projections or regretful reflections. Similarly, gratitude practice fosters a positive mindset that buffers against negativity. Over time, individuals who regularly engage in these practices report greater emotional stability, as they are better equipped to manage their reactions to external stressors. This resilience not only enhances personal well-being but also improves interpersonal relationships, as it allows for more thoughtful, measured responses to others.

Another significant benefit is improved mental clarity and decision-making. Mindfulness, in particular, encourages a sharpened focus and a more discerning perspective. By cultivating the ability to observe thoughts without judgment, individuals can better distinguish between fleeting emotions and genuine insights, leading to wiser, more deliberate choices. Gratitude also contributes by shifting focus toward the positive aspects of situations, helping to identify opportunities that might otherwise be overlooked. When combined with a growing sense of self-confidence, these practices foster a mindset of proactivity and problem-solving, empowering individuals to make decisions with greater confidence and optimism.

Sustained practice also promotes a more positive self-image and deeper self-compassion. As individuals regularly engage in confidence-building exercises and affirmations, they begin to internalize a sense of self-worth that is independent of external validation. This self-assurance is not simply about feeling good in moments of success but about trusting in one's intrinsic value, even in times of failure or criticism. By repeatedly acknowledging and appreciating personal strengths and achievements, individuals build a stable foundation of self-esteem, enabling them to take on challenges with a growth-oriented mindset.

The long-term effects of these practices ripple out into all areas of life. Enhanced resilience, mental clarity, and self-assurance enrich both personal and professional relationships, increase productivity, and cultivate a greater sense of purpose and fulfillment. Life's challenges still arise, but with the benefits of sustained practice, individuals find themselves better equipped to face them, drawing from a deep reservoir of inner strength and positivity. As mindfulness, gratitude, and confidence become ingrained in their daily lives, readers are empowered to lead with intention, respond with compassion, and navigate their paths with a steady sense of purpose and peace.

Key Takeaways and Inspiring the Next Steps for Growth

As we arrive at the end of this book, it's essential to reflect on the path we've traveled together. The journey began with a simple yet powerful idea: insecurity, though common, is not insurmountable. We explored how insecurity subtly infiltrates our professional lives, shaping our decisions, limiting our potential, and holding us back from achieving the careers we deserve. By acknowledging this often-overlooked barrier, we opened the door to understanding its origins, its manifestations, and, most importantly, its solutions.

In the early chapters, we uncovered the roots of insecurity, diving into the psychological and social factors that contribute to feelings of self-doubt and inadequacy. We discussed how imposter syndrome, perfectionism, and fear of failure often intertwine, creating a narrative that convinces us we are less capable than we truly are. This understanding was a crucial step, allowing us to separate fact from fiction and identify where insecurity takes hold in our lives.

From there, we shifted focus to actionable strategies for overcoming insecurity. Each chapter provided tools and techniques tailored to different aspects of professional life, from navigating workplace dynamics and addressing feedback to cultivating a growth mindset and building self-confidence. These practical approaches were not just theoretical but designed to be implemented in real-world scenarios, ensuring that readers could immediately begin making meaningful changes in their lives.

Throughout this journey, one central theme emerged: growth is possible when we face our fears with awareness and intention. The lessons we've explored are not quick fixes but lifelong practices. By consistently applying mindfulness, gratitude, and self-compassion, and by committing to stepping out of our comfort zones, we can gradually transform insecurity from a roadblock into a stepping stone. As we revisit these lessons, the key takeaway is clear: the power to change lies within us, and every small step forward is a victory worth celebrating.

THE COMMON THREAD OF AWARENESS AND ACTION

At the heart of overcoming insecurity lies a critical connection: awareness and action. These two elements, when intertwined, form the foundation for lasting growth and self-assurance. While awareness helps us identify the patterns of insecurity that hold us back, action propels us forward, transforming insight into tangible progress. This dual approach has been a recurring theme throughout the book, underscoring that meaningful change is neither passive nor accidental—it requires both reflection and effort.

Awareness begins with recognizing the subtle yet pervasive ways insecurity manifests in our professional lives. Whether it's hesitating to voice an idea in a meeting, avoiding opportunities for fear of failure, or overcompensating through perfectionism, insecurity often thrives in the shadows of unexamined thoughts and behaviors. By bringing these patterns into the light, we gain clarity about their origins and triggers. This clarity is not about self-criticism but about self-understanding—acknowledging where we are so we can decide where we want to go.

However, awareness alone is not enough. Without action, it risks becoming a source of frustration or inertia. This is where the strategies and tools outlined in the book come into play. Action requires deliberate, incremental steps to challenge insecurity's grip. Whether it's practicing mindfulness to quiet self-doubt, using gratitude to shift focus from shortcomings to strengths, or setting realistic goals to build confidence, each action reinforces the awareness we've cultivated, turning knowledge into empowerment.

Together, awareness and action create a positive feedback loop. The more we act on what we understand about our insecurities, the more we strengthen our ability to confront them. Each small victory, whether it's speaking up in a meeting or embracing constructive feedback, builds momentum. Over time, this loop not only diminishes insecurity but also cultivates a deeper sense of self-trust and resilience. This common thread of awareness and action is the key to lasting growth, reminding us that while insecurity may never fully disappear, we have the tools to rise above it.

TURNING INSIGHTS INTO ACTION

Understanding insecurity and its impact is only the first step; true transformation comes when insights are translated into deliberate, consistent action. Knowledge, no matter how profound, remains static without the willingness to apply it in real-world situations. This chapter of our journey emphasizes the importance of moving from reflection to implementation, empowering readers to use the tools they've acquired to create meaningful change in their lives.

The initial barrier to action is often the fear of failure or imperfection—ironically, the very manifestations of insecurity we aim to overcome. To combat this, it's important to start small. For example, a reader who has recognized their fear of speaking up at work might set an initial goal of contributing a single idea during a team meeting. This seemingly modest step is significant; it marks the beginning of a shift from passivity to participation. Each small action reinforces the message that growth doesn't demand perfection, only persistence.

A practical way to maintain momentum is to establish routines that integrate the insights from this book into daily life. Consistent practices, such as journaling about moments of self-questioning, reflecting on daily successes, or practicing gratitude, transform abstract concepts into tangible habits. Over time, these habits build resilience and self-awareness, enabling readers to confront insecurity with greater confidence. Routines also provide a structured way to measure progress, reminding readers that growth is a process rather than an event.

It's also crucial to embrace the inevitable missteps along the way. No journey of growth is linear, and setbacks are not failures but opportunities to recalibrate. Readers should be encouraged to approach these moments with curiosity rather than judgment, asking, "What can I learn from this experience?" This mindset reinforces one of the book's central themes: challenges, including those we face internally, are opportunities for growth.

By turning insights into action, readers are taking ownership of their development. They move from understanding insecurity to actively dismantling it, one decision, one habit, and one step at a time. This process is empowering not only because it builds confidence but also because it affirms their ability to shape their own narratives. The journey from insight to action is a testament to the reader's commitment to personal and professional growth, and it lays the foundation for sustained change in every facet of life.

INSECURITY AS A SHARED HUMAN EXPERIENCE

Insecurity often feels isolating, as though we're alone in our doubts and fears while everyone around us projects confidence and certainty. This illusion of isolation can intensify the hold insecurity has over us, making us hesitant to seek support or take risks. But the truth is that insecurity is one of the most universal aspects of the human experience. Recognizing this shared reality can transform how we perceive our own struggles, offering both solace and strength.

Throughout history and across cultures, some of the most accomplished individuals have openly acknowledged their insecurities. Writers, scientists, entrepreneurs, and leaders have spoken candidly about moments of self-doubt, questioning whether they were good enough or deserving of their successes. Even those at the pinnacle of achievement are not immune to insecurity; they simply learn how to work with it rather than be paralyzed by it. Understanding that insecurity doesn't discriminate—that it touches everyone, regardless of their accomplishments—helps normalize our own experiences.

In the workplace, this shared reality becomes especially important. The hierarchical nature of professional environments can create the illusion that those above us—managers, mentors, or senior leaders—are immune to insecurity. Yet, many of these individuals face similar fears, such as worrying about being exposed as inadequate or struggling to meet expectations. Recognizing this universality can shift our mindset from one of comparison to one of empathy. Instead of feeling diminished by others' perceived confidence, we can appreciate that everyone is navigating their own challenges.

Acknowledging insecurity as a shared experience also opens the door to connection. When we're honest about our struggles, we encourage others to do the same, fostering an environment of mutual understanding and support. This can be particularly powerful in team settings, where vulnerability can lead to greater collaboration and trust. By seeing insecurity as a common thread that unites rather than isolates us, we cultivate a sense of community and belonging, which are vital for personal and professional growth.

Ultimately, reframing insecurity as a shared human experience removes its power to isolate and shame. Instead of viewing it as a personal weakness, we can recognize it as an opportunity to connect, grow, and support one another. This perspective doesn't erase insecurity, but it does transform how we relate to it, allowing us to face it with greater courage and compassion.

A CALL TO OWNERSHIP

As this journey draws to a close, it's time to reflect on a fundamental truth: no one else can take responsibility for your growth. The tools, insights, and strategies shared in this book are here to guide and support you, but the power to transform your life ultimately lies in your hands. This is the essence of ownership—embracing the idea that your career, confidence, and future are shaped by the actions you choose to take today.

Ownership begins with acknowledging where you are right now. It's not about judgment or self-criticism but about accepting your current reality with honesty and courage. Perhaps insecurity has been holding you back from seeking a promotion, voicing your ideas, or exploring new opportunities. Recognizing these patterns is the first step toward change, because you cannot overcome what you refuse to confront. Ownership means looking inward and taking stock of what you can control—your mindset, your responses, and your willingness to grow.

Taking ownership also involves letting go of excuses and shifting away from a victim mentality. While external factors—like workplace dynamics or societal expectations—can influence feelings of insecurity, they don't have to define your trajectory. Blaming circumstances may feel comforting in the moment, but it also keeps you stuck. True ownership requires asking yourself empowering questions: "What can I do differently? How can I take the first step?" These questions shift the focus from what's outside your control to what's firmly within your grasp.

Action is where ownership truly comes to life. It's not enough to understand your insecurity or recognize its roots; growth requires consistent effort. Whether it's practicing mindfulness, setting boundaries, or embracing feedback, each deliberate step strengthens your confidence and autonomy. Ownership is not about making perfect choices every time—it's about showing up for yourself, even when it's uncomfortable or inconvenient. It's about being accountable to your goals and trusting that your efforts, however small, are moving you forward.

As you move forward, remember that ownership is an ongoing commitment. It's not a destination you reach but a mindset you cultivate daily. By taking ownership, you reclaim your agency and redefine your relationship with insecurity. You no longer wait for permission or perfect conditions to grow;

instead, you create opportunities, embrace challenges, and pave your own path to success. This is your journey, and only you can decide how far you'll go.

Insecurity is Common but Conquerable with the Right Mindset and Tools

Insecurity is a feeling we all encounter at some point in our lives. It transcends age, gender, cultural background, and professional status, uniting us in a shared human experience. Yet, despite its ubiquity, insecurity often isolates us, convincing us that our struggles are unique or indicative of some personal failing. This perception amplifies the discomfort, making it harder to address and overcome. Understanding insecurity as a universal challenge is the first step in breaking its hold.

Throughout history, even the most accomplished individuals have experienced insecurity. Innovators, artists, and leaders have confessed to feelings of self-doubt and inadequacy. Consider Maya Angelou, who, despite her literary and cultural achievements, once said, *"I have written eleven books, but each time I think, 'Uh-oh, they're going to find out now. I've run a game on everybody, and they're going to find me out.'"* Stories like these remind us that insecurity isn't a sign of failure—it's a natural response to stepping into new and uncertain territory.

The illusion of perfection perpetuated by social and professional environments often deepens insecurity. Social media, for example, inundates us with curated images of success, making it easy to believe that everyone else has it together. In reality, the confident colleague, the poised public speaker, or the seemingly unshakeable leader likely face their own moments of doubt. Recognizing this can help dissolve the isolation that insecurity fosters, replacing it with empathy and connection.

Seeing insecurity as a shared experience also opens the door to collective growth. When we acknowledge our own struggles and speak openly about them, we create a culture where others feel safe to do the same. In teams and organizations, this transparency fosters collaboration and trust. In personal relationships, it deepens understanding and support. Insecurity, when faced with honesty and courage, can transform from a source of shame into a catalyst for connection and progress.

By understanding insecurity as a universal challenge, readers can begin to dismantle the myths that give it power. It is not a personal flaw but a shared aspect of being human. With this awareness, the journey toward overcoming insecurity becomes less daunting and more attainable, built on the foundation that no one faces this path alone.

THE JOURNEY OF GROWTH: MINDSET AND TOOLS

Overcoming insecurity is not an overnight transformation; it's a journey that unfolds over time, guided by a deliberate shift in mindset and the consistent use of practical tools. The process begins with awareness, progresses through intentional action, and evolves into sustainable change. Each step reinforces the idea that while insecurity may arise, it does not have to dictate our choices or define our potential.

Central to this journey is the adoption of a growth mindset—the belief that abilities and confidence can be cultivated through effort and learning. This mindset allows us to view insecurity not as a fixed flaw but as an opportunity for self-improvement. By reframing setbacks as lessons and doubts as challenges to overcome, we rewire our thinking, replacing self-limiting beliefs with empowering perspectives. The growth mindset transforms insecurity from an obstacle into a catalyst for progress.

The tools shared throughout this book act as stepping stones along this path. From exercises in mindfulness to strategies for reframing negative thoughts, each tool builds upon the last, creating a comprehensive framework for managing insecurity. For example, journaling helps uncover hidden fears, while practicing gratitude fosters a more balanced self-image. Together, these tools don't just address the symptoms of insecurity—they tackle its root causes, providing a foundation for lasting confidence.

Consistent practices, such as journaling about moments of self-criticism, reflecting on daily successes, or practicing gratitude, transform abstract concepts into tangible habits. But with a mindset that embraces progress over perfection, and with tools ready to support us, these moments become manageable. The key is persistence—showing up for yourself even on the days when insecurity feels overwhelming. Over time, these small, intentional actions accumulate, leading to profound transformation.

The journey of growth is deeply personal, but it's not one that has to be walked alone. Whether through mentors, supportive colleagues, or shared vulnerability with friends, the insights and encouragement of others can amplify our efforts. By combining the right mindset with actionable tools and a commitment to consistency, the path forward becomes not just attainable but inspiring. Insecurity may always linger on the edges, but its grip loosens as we step confidently into our potential.

ENVISIONING A LIFE BEYOND INSECURITY

Imagine a version of yourself no longer defined by the persistent grip of insecurity—a self that steps into challenges with confidence, speaks up without fear of judgment, and embraces opportunities without the shadow of self-doubt. This is not a distant, unattainable ideal; it is a tangible outcome of sustained growth and self-awareness. To move forward, it's crucial to visualize what life beyond insecurity can look like and understand the freedom it offers.

A life beyond insecurity is one where your decisions are guided by aspirations rather than anxieties. Instead of hesitating at the edge of an opportunity, fearing you're not ready or capable, you step forward with the assurance that growth comes through action. In this new mindset, rejection or failure becomes a temporary detour rather than an endpoint, empowering you to explore paths you once avoided. Each choice you make, no matter how small, is a reflection of your belief in your own potential.

Professional growth flourishes when insecurity is no longer a dominant force. Imagine negotiating for the raise you deserve, taking the lead on high-profile projects, or transitioning to a new career with clarity and purpose. Without the weight of second-guessing yourself, you can channel your energy into creativity, innovation, and leadership. This shift not only enhances your career trajectory but also elevates your presence and influence in the workplace, inspiring others through your confidence and authenticity.

On a personal level, relationships are transformed as insecurity loosens its hold. When you're no longer consumed by fears of inadequacy or rejection, you can connect with others more openly and authentically. This authenticity deepens bonds, builds trust, and allows for healthier communication. Instead of seeking external validation, you bring self-assurance into your interactions, creating space for mutual growth and understanding.

Envisioning a life beyond insecurity is not about eliminating every trace of self-questioning but about reducing its influence. It's about experiencing the freedom to pursue what matters most without being paralyzed by fear. It's a life where your inner voice is kind and encouraging, where challenges are stepping stones rather than barriers, and where your actions align with your values and ambitions.

This vision is more than motivation; it's a roadmap for what is possible. With the tools, strategies, and mindset cultivated throughout this book, stepping into this version of yourself is not just a dream—it's the inevitable result of your commitment to growth and self-empowerment.

A FINAL EMPOWERING CALL TO ACTION

As we reach the conclusion of this journey, it's time to take the insights and tools shared throughout this book and put them into action. Insecurity, while universal and deeply ingrained, does not have to dictate the course of your life. The power to change lies within you—within the choices you make every day, the mindset you cultivate, and the tools you consistently use. This is your moment to commit to a life shaped not by fear, but by growth and confidence.

The first step is acknowledgment. Recognize that insecurity is not a weakness or a failure but a sign of your humanity. It's the echo of experiences, societal pressures, and self-imposed expectations that no longer serve you. By understanding its roots andf triggers, you gain the awareness necessary to confront it head-on. This awareness is the foundation of transformation; it empowers you to break free from reactive patterns and step into deliberate, purposeful action.

The next step is persistence. Change is not instantaneous, and setbacks are inevitable. But each small, intentional step forward—whether it's practicing gratitude, reframing a negative thought, or speaking up in a meeting—creates momentum. Over time, these small victories accumulate, building the confidence and resilience necessary to tackle larger challenges. Remember, growth is not about perfection; it's about progress. Celebrate each step forward, no matter how small, as evidence of your commitment to becoming the best version of yourself.

Finally, embrace ownership of your journey. While insecurity may have been shaped by external forces, its resolution lies within your control. You have the tools to rewrite your narrative, to quiet the inner critic, and to redefine your relationship with self-doubt. This doesn't mean insecurity will never arise again—it likely will. But when it does, you'll have the mindset and strategies to face it, reducing its impact and moving forward with clarity and confidence.

As you close this book, envision the life you want to lead and the person you aspire to be. You now have the knowledge and tools to bridge the gap between where you are and where you want to go. The path will not always be easy, but it will always be worth it. Take the first step today—start that journal, take that risk, have that conversation. Every action you take brings you closer to a life of purpose, fulfillment, and confidence.

The journey doesn't end here. It's ongoing, evolving as you grow and learn. But now, you embark on it equipped with the mindset and tools to conquer insecurity and embrace the limitless potential within you. This is your call to action—step boldly into your future, knowing that you are capable, resilient, and deserving of every success.

Discover more

Author

Other books

www.ingramcontent.com/pod-product-compliance
Lightning Source LLC
Chambersburg PA
CBHW071505220526
45472CB00003B/918